How to
AVOID
PROBATE
for Everyone

Protecting Your Estate
for Your Loved Ones

T0001820

RONALD FARRINGTON SHARP

ALLWORTH PRESS
NEW YORK

Allworth Press books may be purchased in bulk at special discounts for sales promotion, corporate gifts, fund-raising, or educational purposes. Special editions can also be created to specifications. For details, contact the Special Sales Department, Allworth Press, 307 West 36th Street, 11th Floor, New York, NY 10018 or info@skyhorsepublishing.com.

24 23 22 21 20   5 4 3 2 1

Published by Allworth Press, an imprint of Skyhorse Publishing, Inc. 307 West 36th Street, 11th Floor, New York, NY 10018.

Allworth Press® is a registered trademark of Skyhorse Publishing, Inc.®, a Delaware corporation.

www.allworth.com

Cover design by Mary Belibasakis

Library of Congress Cataloging-in-Publication Data

Names: Sharp, Ronald Farrington, author.
Title: How to avoid probate for everyone: protecting your estate for your loved ones / Ronald Farrington Sharp.
Description: New York: Allworth Press, 2020. | Includes index.
Identifiers: LCCN 2019050256 (print) | LCCN 2019050257 (ebook) | ISBN 9781621537304 (trade paperback) | ISBN 9781621537311 (epub)
Subjects: LCSH: Probate law and practice—United States—Popular works. | Estate planning—United States—Popular works. | Trusts and trustees—United States—Popular works. | LCGFT: Legal forms.
Classification: LCC KF765 .S53 2020 (print) | LCC KF765 (ebook) | DDC 346.7305/2--dc23
LC record available at https://lccn.loc.gov/2019050256
LC ebook record available at https://lccn.loc.gov/2019050257

Print ISBN: 978-1-62153-730-4
eBook ISBN: 978-1-62153-731-1

Printed in the United States of America

"Death is not the end. There remains the litigation over the estate."

—Ambrose Bierce, *Epigrams of a Cynic*

Author's Note

This book discusses, but is not limited to, the use of many non-trust ways of avoiding probate as well as trusts as a probate avoidance method. For more detailed information on trust creation and settlement, the book *Living Trusts for Everyone* is another great resource.

Contents

Introduction

Here's what I think about using the probate court to settle a decedent's estate: Probate is an unnecessary evil that can be made necessary because of improper planning. While probate has its uses, it is like an antidote for a snake bite—indispensable if you need it, but something you hope you will never have to use. Better you should avoid snakes—and probate. If you don't mind spending lots of money to pass on your assets to your heirs, and if you like the idea of their waiting for up to two years to inherit— during which time they get to meet with attorneys multiple times and attend court hearings—then probate is for you.

That said, let's talk about what we mean by probate. Probate is a broad term that encompasses all of the functions of a probate court, including settling a decedent's estate as well as myriad other functions involving estates, the disabled, and children. While it is important to avoid the costs and time delays of probate court, we sometimes do need to use the judicial functions and power of the courts to further the wishes of a decedent. It's useful as a backup when we need to protect the interests of a person's heirs. So it's not totally and completely bad.

This book identifies and describes methods of avoiding probate of estates. Books on probate avoidance typically recommend the use of revocable trusts as a will alternative and stop there. Sometimes they even supply a fill-in-the-blank form to make a do-it-yourself trust. However, trusts are not the only way to avoid probate estate administration, and sometimes they are not the best way. The goal of any estate plan should be to ensure that the assets remaining at death are distributed or managed according to the wishes of the deceased in the least complicated, least expensive, and least time-consuming manner. While trusts are good, there are many other ways to avoid probate that do not rely on either a will or a trust. The makeup of a person's assets, their intentions, and their family situation will determine which methods are preferable. These alternate methods and how they work are detailed in the following pages.

The probate court also can interfere in your affairs in non-estate settlement areas. For example, there are methods of avoiding probate court involvement in minor or adult conservatorships. Probate courts can take administrative control of the assets of minor children and mentally disabled adults to protect their money from loss or misuse, but this service comes with several burdens. There are significant costs to these estates for the fees of a guardian-ad-litem and court-appointed conservators. The court has the discretion to and may well appoint someone other than your first choice to serve in these roles. If a family member or friend is appointed, they will be forced to file reports and paperwork and attend regular court hearings, which might require them to take time off work and/or pay an attorney. Proper planning can keep the court out of your family affairs.

The judicial functions of a court can be utilized if needed to help collect assets of the estate or to enforce the terms of estate administration without subjecting the entire estate to court oversight.

The appendices include sample documents so that you can see what they typically look like. I do not recommend that you copy these for your own use. They may or may not be appropriate for your situation or in your home state. This is not a textbook or treatise on the law, and laws vary among the states, so do not rely on this as legal or tax advice for your particular situation. You should consult a lawyer in your individual jurisdiction to effectuate any legal plan that you need.

I think you will find the information herein helpful.

—Ronald Farrington Sharp

CHAPTER ONE

The Probate Process

What exactly is probate? Historically, the word *probate* is the process of filing a decedent's will with a court and "proving it." The proof required is, first, that it is the most recent true will of the person signing it, and second, that the person was of sound mind and not under undue influence when it was signed. The proof traditionally required was the testimony of two witnesses who saw it being signed. But wills can be found valid even without witnesses if, for example, it is written in the handwriting of the will maker (holographic will), but proving such a will most often requires a court hearing and the testimony of interested parties.

Nowadays a will can be self-proving without a hearing or witness testimony by following the local statute, which usually requires that the will also be notarized. Then the probate process begins. Probate procedures are statutory: they are codified into written law in each state. The particular court may be called Probate Court, but might also have another name, such as Superior Court or Circuit Court. The point is that the state court system is in charge of the probate process, which follows a step-by-step procedure as laid out in the written laws. In this book, the applicable court will be referred to as the probate court.

This kind of thing has happened in my office many times: A client comes to me complaining that the real estate people won't let her sell her deceased father's house even though she is the only child, Mom is dead, and the will leaves everything to her. She also can't access his bank accounts even after giving a copy of the will to the bank manager. Logically and morally, she should be right. But the problem is that the real estate companies and banks want to protect themselves and be sure that the will is valid, that it has not been revoked, and that there is some court authority on which they can hang their hats before allowing the daughter access to the assets. Can't blame them for that. In this situation, some sort of probate is necessary so that there is a court order signed by a judge that confirms that she is entitled to the house and accounts.

A person in possession of a will is required to turn it over to the court upon the death of its maker. The court then appoints a named personal representative or an appointed administrator to shepherd the will through the process of gathering all assets together, paying all debts and expenses, and distributing the remainder to the heirs named in the will according to its instructions.

This should be simple, but it is not. And it can be incredibly expensive and time-consuming.

But what if there is no will? According to LexisNexis, 55 percent of people die without either a will or a trust. Sometimes they assume everything will somehow magically work out the way they expect. Most people, I think, have in the back of their minds that they should have a will or some other kind of estate plan, but never get around to doing it. They may expect that probate will be involved and that there is nothing they need to do to expedite things. Isn't it really a problem for the heirs?

If you don't decide on an estate plan for yourself, your state laws have already made one for you. Not having an estate plan is somewhat like not voting. The law assumes that you must not care what happens and are willing to accept whatever everyone else decides; otherwise you would have done something about it.

The laws determining who gets what when a person dies without a will are called the laws of descent and distribution (or, the laws of intestacy). These state laws lay out the respective shares of the heirs of the deceased and depend upon whether the person was married or had children, or both. They vary from state to state, but the laws are similar. The text of the law in Appendix A is a typical example from Michigan, but a simple internet search for "descent and distribution" with the addition of your state's name will give you specifics for your state.

Making your own plan to leave your assets at your death, by will or otherwise, can also avoid unintended inheritances. Suppose you have no children and your spouse dies, leaving business assets or accounts that were in her name alone. According to the rules in Michigan you would get *"The first $150,000.00, plus 3/4 of any balance of the intestate estate, if no descendant of the decedent survives the decedent, but a parent of the decedent survives the decedent."* Do you really want to share your spouse's separate estate with your mother-in-law? Most of us assume our spouse would be entitled to our assets if we die without a will, but that is just not always true.

Another typical situation: Your spouse has children, but none of them are your children, and then your spouse dies. In this case you would get the first $100,000 of his assets and one-half of the rest. This can create severe hardship on a surviving spouse who had been counting on all the assets for his or her support and maintenance for life.

Now, if you and your spouse jointly own everything and are each other's beneficiaries, it is true there would be no probate at the death of one of you because there are no separately owned assets remaining at the death of the first spouse. But what if you each have separate assets, like business or partnership interests or private bank or investment accounts? In that case the intestacy laws apply. And at the death of the survivor, probate would likely be inevitable, and your heirs will not only get just a partial share but will be shouldering the costs of probate as well.

Try not to die intestate unless you agree with the state intestacy rules. Making sure your intentions are followed as to the distribution of your estate at death is important, but not forcing your spouse or children to go through the expensive and time-consuming probate process is equally important.

Unmarried couples in particular must have a will or a probate-avoiding estate plan. Without a recognized legal marriage, the couple does not have spousal rights as set out in the statutes. This can lead to disinheriting your companion. A will, trust, or other plan can avoid this unfortunate situation. I have seen a surviving unmarried partner be forced out of a house he had lived in for thirty years by the children of the first partner to die, since the house had been owned only in the deceased partner's name. He died and the house now belongs to the deceased partner's children. Planning is everything.

An important point is that in nearly all states it is impossible to totally disinherit a spouse by use of a will. The surviving spouse typically has a right to either take what was left to him or her in the will or take what the state statutes would allow instead: a "forced share" of the total probate estate. There are also rules permitting a spousal allowance to be paid prior to the closing of probate. Interestingly, in many states the deceased can disinherit a spouse through a living trust, but not through a will. So, there's another reason to avoid probate if you are not inclined to take care of your spouse. This is also important for separated or estranged couples with separate assets.

Can't the state make a regular will for you so you don't have to deal with intestacy laws? In fact, some states have a state-promulgated "statutory will." This is a fill-in-the-blank will form available from the state, so that those without wills can get one without having to pay a lawyer. But it is still a will, and while in some cases it is better than no will at all, it still has to be probated if assets are to pass through it to your heirs.

There are other areas of your life where probate court can make things difficult if you let them. You might not want the court involved in managing your money and medical care decisions should you become incompetent because of Alzheimer's or dementia. You might also prefer someone other than a court-appointed conservator to manage the inheritance going to your minor children until their adulthood. We can avoid the courts in those situations just as we can avoid the court supervision of estates.

Typically, in the civil areas, the probate court handles the estates of deceased persons as well as adult and children guardianships and conservatorships, adoptions, and foster care. They might also handle juvenile criminal cases and termination of parental rights. This can vary from state to state, but for purposes of this book we will be concerned only with probated estates, guardianships, and conservatorships.

WHY AVOID PROBATE?

First, by avoiding probate you avoid the **time** it takes to complete the probate process. This is important because the entire process can take months or years to complete before all the assets are finally distributed to the rightful heirs. Creditors have to be given notice of the death and have an opportunity to prove the amount they are owed from the estate. There are sometimes minimum waiting periods set by law before an estate can be closed. All this waiting means that the heirs have to wait before there is a complete distribution of the remaining estate assets to them. It is their money, but not until the court says so.

Then there is the time involved for your family. Meetings with lawyers. Court time, which in most cases ends up taking half a day per hearing due to travel time and waiting your turn in front of the judge. Probate court is often a cattle-call, with dozens of cases scheduled for the same hearing time and date. Taking time off work is usually required—not the way most of us want to spend a vacation or personal day. These all add up.

The time delay also exacerbates family relations. The longer the process takes, the more impatient people get. *Maybe we should have our own lawyer*, they each might think.

Whenever there is more than one lawyer, there are going to be additional costs and problems. The new lawyers have to show they are doing something to earn their fees, so the mud gets stirred up.

Second, **privacy** is an issue. Court documents are public record unless the judge, in an unusual move, seals them. Anyone can take a look at the will and other paperwork, and even receive copies. They can find out who the heirs are, where they live, how much they are inheriting, and who may have been included or excluded. This information should be private, but if the estate is probated, it isn't. Beneficiaries are sometimes subjected to unwanted solicitations from those who watch the probate filings.

When a non-probate settlement method such as a trust is used rather than a will, the only people entitled to a copy of the documents are those who are specifically named in the trust, and even they only get to see the parts that pertain to them. Privacy is an advantage of trusts.

Third, **cost**. Probate is expensive. The number-one cost is not court costs, as people think. It is attorney and executor fees. These can be based on the attorney's hourly rate multiplied by the number of hours she spends on the case, or in some states it can be a percentage of the total value of the assets being probated. In the percentage situation, the amount can be increased if there are issues that require additional time, such as will contests. Money spent on probate is money taken out of your heirs' inheritance. You are paying for it.

Several states have published suggested fees for attorneys and executors that are based upon the gross dollar value of the estate (*before* deduction of debts owed, such as mortgages). Here is the chart relied upon by Florida attorneys to determine their fees as set out in Florida law. Also, keep in mind that the executor will often expect the same compensation.

Compensable Value of Estate	Attorney Compensation
$40,000.00 or less	$1,500
$40,000.01 to $70,000.00	$2,250
$70,000.01 to $100,000.00	$3,000
$100,000.01 to $1,000,000.00	$3,000; plus 3% on the value of estate from $100,000.01 to $1,000,000.00
$1,000,000.01 to $3,000,000.00	$3,000; plus 3% on the value of estate from $100,000.01 to $1,000,000.00; plus 2.5% on the value of the estate from $1,000,000.01 to $3,000,000.00
$3,000,000.01 to $5,000,000.00	$3,000; plus 3% on the value of estate from $100,000.01 to $1,000,000.00; plus 2.5% on the value of the estate from $1,000,000.01 to $3,000,000.00; plus 2% on the value of the estate from $3,000,000.01 to $5,000,000.00
$5,000,000.01 to $10,000,000.00	$3,000; plus 3% on the value of estate from $100,000.01 to $1,000,000.00; plus 2.5% on the value of the estate from $1,000,000.01 to $3,000,000.00; plus 2% on the value of the estate from $3,000,000.01 to $5,000,000.00; plus 1.5% on the value of the estate from $5,000,000.01 to $10,000,000.00

(Continued on next page)

Compensable Value of Estate	Attorney Compensation
$10,000,000.01 or above	$3,000; plus 3% on the value of estate from $100,000.01 to $1,000,000.00; plus 2.5% on the value of the estate from $1,000,000.01 to $3,000,000.00; plus 2% on the value of the estate from $3,000,000.01 to $5,000,000.00; plus 1.5% on the value of the estate from $5,000,000.01 to $10,000,000.00; plus 1% on the value of the estate above $10,000,000.00

Note that this fee schedule is not necessarily related to the amount of work done, since it may take no more work to administer a $2 million estate than a $100,000 one, though the fees would be vastly different. These are suggestions and not rules, so the attorney may end up charging much more than the schedule but rarely less. Most people don't realize that attorney fees are negotiable, though many lawyers won't vary from the chart at a minimum. You should always get a written and signed fee agreement.

The other ways to charge for attorney fees are a flat rate or an hourly rate. Hourly is most common, preferred by lawyers, and can add up fast. With fees ranging from $150 to $600 per hour or more, depending upon the attorney and location of the courthouse, the hourly rate is a great moneymaker for lawyers—often the resulting charges exceed the state suggestions. That fifteen-minute court hearing might cost you several hours when you add in travel time, research, waiting time in court, telephone calls, and document preparation. It really is possible to get a flat rate attorney fee, but most attorneys shy away from that. They are under pressure, particularly in large firms, to bill hours and maximize their fees.

I have had estate planning attorneys tell me that I am wrong about the cost of probate. They say that the costs of probate and the costs of a trust are comparable. When I asked how much they charged for a trust and for trust settlement (which is carrying out the instructions of the trust—most of which is not legal work but is charged as such), I was not surprised at their conclusion. They were charging a lot for probate, which was not unusual, but would charge just as much for a trust, settlement of the trust, and preparation of the related documents. One attorney a few years ago said his office used a performance-based fee structure, charging a percentage of how much they saved a client in estate taxes. This was back when many clients had to worry about the estate tax because the exemption threshold was so low. So, yeah, he was right, mainly due to his exorbitant fee structure. There are some attorneys who will quote a reasonable flat rate for a trust and all the related documents. Shop around.

Court costs are also very significant, if not as expensive as the attorney fees. The administrator, executor, or personal representative is entitled to a fee, sometimes on the same basis as the attorney—again, itemized hourly or a percentage. Guardians may be appointed for minor children beneficiaries, and they are also paid from the estate funds and are often attorneys as well.

There are other court costs, including filing fees, bond fees, and an inventory fee. The inventory fee is a percentage of the total estate value, which goes to the court. In most cases, this is based on the value of the asset without deduction for debt. So, on a $200,000 house with a $150,000 mortgage, the inventory fee is charged against the $200,000. Sounds like a tax, doesn't it? Any time I write a check to the government, to me it's a tax by another name. All these fees are eliminated if you avoid probating the estate. How to do so is revealed in the following chapters.

Fourth, **litigation**. Opening a probate case means that a court case has been filed. It has a court file number, a judge is assigned, and there are generally preprinted or downloadable forms to cover nearly any sort of issue that might arise. If an heir does not believe a will is valid then it is quite easy to contest the will, since the court file already exists. Contesting a will can be close to extortion, since the mere fact of filing an objection, no matter how specious, means that there will be vast amounts of attorney time, and thus attorney fees, paid to sort out the complaint. Even if a claim or challenge is unsuccessful, the heirs lose anyway because the estate attorney's fees come off the top before any distribution is made to the heirs. Sometimes it is easier and cheaper to just make a cash settlement with the person contesting rather than go through lengthy and expensive legal proceedings. Sure, it's wrong, but that's the way things work.

CONTESTING A WILL

Wills can be legitimately contested for many reasons. Was the deceased subject to undue influence, say by an unrelated nurse, girlfriend, or companion who ended up in the will? Is a child of the deceased disinherited without apparent cause? Perhaps the deceased was suffering from some form of dementia at the time the will was made. Does the will violate the terms of a divorce judgment or prenuptial agreement? These can be questions of fact that require a formal trial and presentation of evidence for the judge to determine the validity of the will. And again, it is easy to do, since the court case has been filed and already exists. Plus, the fees of both sides are often paid out of the estate, so the person contesting has nothing to lose.

Suppose you have a child from hell and there is no way you want the kid to inherit anything from you. If you make out a will and just leave their name off, he or she will be able to inherit anyway. The assumption is that you would not have omitted the object of your affection, so it must have been a mistake. An oversight. The child would be what the law calls a pretermitted heir. Even if you specifically state that it is your intention to leave nothing to Johnny under any circumstance, he can still contest it using various theories, such as that you were mentally incompetent or under duress when you excluded him. We do not want a will probated that could be contested by Johnny. Using a trust or another method avoids most court problems.

Probate-avoiding methods such as trusts can be contested in court, of course, but it is much more difficult. First, the person contesting has to find a lawyer and pay a hefty retainer fee. They don't take these kinds of cases on a contingency basis. They must pay court filing and service of process fees. You have to pay for the court challenge whether you win or lose. It is an hourly rate that adds up fast. There are no fill-in-the-blank forms for this type of lawsuit, so the paperwork has to be especially written, which takes more time.

Most trusts contain a disinheritance clause, which says that if anyone contests the trust, they are either disinherited or their share is limited to one dollar. While this provision is not necessarily always enforceable, it discourages people from litigation. Arbitration clauses are also usually added to trusts, which also limit the options for a contestant.

Probate and its attendant costs and time delays is a certainty for those with assets that remain in their own name at the time of their death. Making a will doesn't change the length of time probate takes or its costs. In both cases, will or no will, probate will be necessary to transfer the assets remaining to the rightful heirs. And the probate process is neither simpler nor shorter just because you have a will. The common misconception is that a will solves all the problems, but that is just not true. There are non-probate alternatives that we will explore in this book that eliminate most of the expense and time of the probate process.

Of course, the number-one most effective never-fail way of avoiding probate is the plan recommended by the former billionaire Jorge Guinle: "The secret of living well is to die without a cent in your pocket. But I miscalculated, and the money ran out too early." Proper estate and financial planning is a must.

Again, a will is not the way to avoid probate. However, a will might still be needed even when there is no probatable estate. There are several reasons why this seeming contradiction is correct.

When a person dies leaving minor children but no living parent, a will is absolutely necessary to ensure that the children wind up living with a guardian of the parents' choice.

Wills prepared for parents with minor children (even pour-over wills, which are described later) should always contain a provision appointing a guardian for minor children. Ideally, first and second choices are nominated in case the first choice is unable to be the guardian. Couples are not recommended since we have no idea if they will still be married at the time of the parents' deaths. Naming a couple could lead to a custody battle between the two of them in the future. A first and second and even third choice of nominated individuals is best.

Your choice of guardian can be contested by other relatives despite your having put your choices in your will, but the named guardians will have preference to a judge unless they can be shown to be unfit to the point that they are not in the best interests of the children (again, depending on local state law). A guardianship is necessary in order to have someone fill the parental roles of raising the children. Feeding, clothing, housing, discipline, religion, education, and things like when they can date or drive a car. The guardian is in charge of all those decisions and medical care as well. The children's expenses, however, would likely be paid to the guardian through the child's conservatorship account or, we hope, their trust funds.

A conservator is the court-appointed person(s) who manages the child's money if there is no trust. If the parents did not set up a trust with a trustee, then the court will appoint a conservator who has to account periodically to the court for what has been spent and earned on the account. Sometimes the guardian and conservator are the same person, and sometimes not. Someone might be very good at raising children but not so good in financial matters, and vice versa. Your choice of these two people has to take that into account.

You can appoint a conservator in your will in the same paragraph that you name the guardian and should have alternate choices for that job as well. It is also recommended that two people serve together as conservator, since it ensures that the asset management is done efficiently and honestly.

CHAPTER TWO

Avoiding Probate without Using Trusts: Simplified and Summary Probate

The number-one solution to avoiding probate put forth by estate planners and most books on the subject is the creation of a living trust. I have no argument with this and have done thousands of trusts myself for clients. My book, *Living Trusts for Everyone*, concentrates on this solution. But lots of people can avoid probate with even simpler methods by avoiding the possible cost and complexity that comes with a trust.

Critics of my strong advice to avoid probate typically have two arguments. First, they say that probate isn't really all that bad, and in fact protects the heirs. Second, they say that there are already procedures in place through the courts to shortcut the probate process for simple low-asset estates with typical distribution plans. Those arguments have some merit in very limited cases. These court procedures are simpler than full-blown probate, but still involve a court process. There are even simpler ways to avoid even summary and small estate court procedures.

California, for example, allows for a quick assignment of assets to a decedent's heirs if the total assets do not exceed $100,000. It is possible to use this procedure without an attorney, but it's not simple. Other states, such as Michigan, have the threshold at $22,000. Many states have similar thresholds and procedures, but there are fees and paperwork that apply and an attorney is often required to push the paperwork through. Also, some of these transfers of ownership through the simplified plans are not recognized or accepted by real estate title insurance companies and financial institutions, so the estate might have to be fully probated anyway.

The Superior Court in California, which handles probate cases, offers instructions on how to use the simplified process in that state. The "simple" instructions are eleven pages of single-spaced type. And as to real estate, the "simplified" process applies only to property valued at less than $50,000 or less than $150,000, depending upon the procedure. I don't know how many homes and real estate are in that valuation range, but given that the average price of California real estate is $525,000 according to Zillow.com, I expect few people qualify. The procedure also requires that all the heirs consent to the assignments using the process, which might not be in line with the wishes of the deceased. If they don't consent, there might be a full-blown probate anyway.

Another good example is the affidavit procedure in Texas. There are several small estate procedures, as follows:

1. Affidavit of Heirship. This is available if there was no will and the only remaining asset is real estate. All the legal heirs at law must agree to the affidavit, which has several requirements, including that the deceased had no debts at death. Someone (presumably an attorney) has to figure out how to write the affidavit to comply with the law, and after it is signed, witnessed, and notarized, it is filed with the local recorder of deeds. Sounds pretty simple, but the problem is that many real estate title companies and banks do not view the affidavit as a legal transfer of title and will require probate before that property can be mortgaged or sold.

2. Small Estate Affidavit. This is similar to the affidavit of heirship, except it does not apply to real estate, and the

assets other than real estate must be less than $50,000, with all heirs agreeing on the assignment of these assets to them. This is filed with the probate court, but there is no court hearing. There are fees that apply. Again, those institutions servicing bank and brokerage accounts as well as other investments will often refuse to accept the affidavit and will require a probate court order before they hand over the funds.

3. Muniment of Title. This allows the transfer of real estate to named heirs under a will by using an affidavit. It does not apply to any other kind of property. The real estate must be specifically described and given to the heirs in the will, and there can be no debt owed on the property. This procedure is handled in the probate court but has limited use due to its requirements. It is a probate process.

There are a lot of states that have similar small estate summary probate proceedings. These laws were enacted after the legislatures recognized the public demand for less complicated and inexpensive ways to transfer the assets of a decedent to his or her heirs. Unfortunately, as described above, the solutions adopted are sometimes complicated too and apply only to certain proscribed types and sizes of estates.

For another example, there are probate laws in some states that allow for so-called independent or unsupervised probate procedures. These have some advantages over regular supervised probate in that each and every decision during the administrative process does not have to be approved by a judge. However, the time constraints still apply as well as the court fees and taxes. The attorney fees may also be less, but the fact is that it is still a probate court process with all the other disadvantages and costs.

Attorneys have the option in Michigan and some other states as to which probate process they will use for an estate. Those whose interest is in maximizing attorney fees and not in a quick and cheap independent process will opt for the paper-work and court appearances in heavily supervised administra-tion, even though the unsupervised process would work just as well. Clients will not know the difference. Just sayin'.

Later in this book, I will describe inexpensive ways of han-dling estates, regardless of size, that will allow you to bypass the probate courts entirely.

WHEN YOU NEED PROBATE, BUT JUST A LITTLE ONE: PARTIAL PROBATE

In certain situations, probate might be necessary at least for part of the assets of an estate. Even with proper planning, where most of a person's assets are being handled by probate-avoiding devices such as a revocable trust, the power of the court system can be tapped by putting some of the estate assets through the system.

Suppose there are assets of the deceased that need to be collected but those who have them refuse to turn them over, dispute the value of them, or hide information on their exis-tence or whereabouts. Probate courts have the authority to issue injunctions, subpoena documents, subpoena witnesses to testify, order receiverships, and even require assets to be turned over to the probated estate. Trials can be held on disputed ques-tions of fact relating to the estate.

It is not unusual to see assets disappear when a person nears death. I have dragged folks in front of the judge to explain what happened to bank balances, personal property, boats, and prac-tically anything that can be carried away. The usual response, after initial denials, is that the deceased intended the items as a gift. Using the court's power, I have been able to get copies of canceled checks and car title transfers to see what actually happened. Follow the paper trail. Without some corroborating evidence of the intent to make a gift, the courts will normally require the assets to be returned to the estate. The closer the alleged gift was made to the date of incompetency or death, the more likely the court is to require a return of the property.

Small business partnerships are very often problems when one partner dies. While a partnership agreement or buy-sell contract would avoid such problems, most small businesses don't have them. The surviving partner might stonewall when pressed for information on assets and debts of the business. It is understandable that the partner would not want the family or heirs of the deceased involved in the business, but the value of the business is rightfully an estate asset. The court can order an examination of the books, appraisals of assets, and even put the business under receivership until the needed information is produced.

Missing documents are another solvable problem. Sometimes we know that a trust was created because we find recorded deeds in the name of the decedent's trust, but no one can find the original trust document. Perhaps it was destroyed by someone who was disinherited. If we know the name of the attorney who wrote the trust it is possible, with the testimony of the lawyer and any witnesses to the signing of the trust, to have the court certify that a photocopy can legally substitute for the missing paperwork. States have lost-document statutes that set out the procedure for creating a valid stand-in for the missing original.

In a case where a trust has been created but no one is willing to act as a trustee to implement the trust provisions, the court can appoint a trustee, usually without subjecting the trust to formal court supervision. This can be more easily done if the trust itself addresses that situation and requests that the court act in a ministerial role to make that appointment. This happens when the named trustees have predeceased the trust maker, or are themselves incompetent, or just don't want to be the trustee. The fact that they were appointed in the trust document does not mean they are required to take on that responsibility. Having a choice can come as a big relief to an appointed trustee who is not also an heir.

The following examples illustrate problems encountered by my clients. Solutions to the problems are identified and described, provided that a solution was possible. Sometimes all I can do is explain what should or could have been done to avoid the problem in the first place. As a way of describing the character roles, I have given the characters aliases, which are by definition not their names in real life.

Example 1

Bob and Elizabeth had worked for years to build up a better than average-sized estate. They had their home mortgage-free and well maintained, as well as various investments including bank and retirement accounts. Their two grown children, Tina and Jerry, were married with their own homes and lived nearby. Being responsible sorts, Bob and Elizabeth went to an attorney recommended by their insurance agent to have their will made. They had read about avoiding probate, so they asked the attorney about the advisability of getting a trust set up. They were considering setting aside some money in trust for their three grandchildren's education and had heard that a trust could accomplish that goal.

Their lawyer knew a bit about wills, probate, and trusts, though he was not a specialist, and thus created wills for them. Included in the language of the wills were several pages devoted to describing the terms of the requested grandchildren's trust and appointing the parents of the grandchildren as the trustees of the trust, as well as personal representatives (executors) of the will itself.

After the deaths of Bob and Elizabeth, Tina and Jerry went back to the lawyer, who had the original wills, expecting a quick and inexpensive settlement of the estate.

Of course, that did not happen, or I would not use this as an example.

The lawyer explained that everything was in order and that he needed some information to prepare the wills for probate and get the trusts set up. The process, he said, was to advertise the notice of probate, notify creditors, inventory the estate assets, pay the probate and creditor expenses, transfer the shares of the children into a court-supervised trust account, and then transfer the remaining assets to Tina and Jerry. The process would take six to twelve months, and he could not estimate the total costs since it would depend upon how much time he expended on it. His hourly rate of $275 was typical for the area, he explained, and in any event, it would have to be approved by the judge.

Tina and Jerry left with their list of information requirements and, after discussing it for a few days, came to see me for a second opinion. Wasn't there an easier and cheaper way out of this?

Had they come to see me instead of the other attorney, I would have created a plan in which there would have been no probate for either the estates or for the trust, and there would have been no attorney fees or court fees at the deaths of Bob and Elizabeth. As it was, the best I could do was offer to do the probate with the understanding that they would participate by doing the non-legal parts of the process. The other attorney released the wills to me, and I prepared the initial paperwork and filed it to begin the process.

Most clients do not understand that much of the work in a probate case is clerical rather than legal. You do not need to pay several hundred dollars an hour for form document preparation or filing things with the court. They agreed to my plan and we were able to reduce the attorney time substantially by having them deal with insurance claims, paperwork, meeting with real estate people and appraisers about the house, arranging for insurance on the property while the estate was pending, and communicating with the financial institutions and other accounts that had named them as beneficiaries, which were not part of the probatable estate.

The trust that was in the will is what we call a testamentary trust (contained within the last will and testament), so it had to remain under supervision of the court. But I showed them how to do the annual accounting for the children's trust funds so that they could avoid paying attorney fees for the pro-forma annual review by the court.

Then both Jerry and Tina came to me to do their own estate plans, which I set up with probate-avoiding plans.

There is no benefit to using a testamentary trust except to the lawyer. From the lawyer's business perspective, using the testamentary trust allows them to bill for the will, the trust preparation, the probate, and the annual legal work for the trust once the probate is completed. Good for the lawyer, not so good for the clients or their heirs. It's not that lawyers doing this are being dishonest or even negligent. More often it is ignorance of probate-avoiding methods and practices.

Don't be Bob and Elizabeth. Be Tina and Jerry.

Example 2

In this case, the lawyer actually created a revocable living trust as a separate stand-alone document for the client. Along with that he set up the ancillary documents, which included a pour-over will. That was the client's undoing.

A living trust may have lots of different functions. It might spread out inheritances over a period of time rather than in a lump sum. It might provide for a lifetime income to a surviving spouse with the remainder to children. It could include charitable bequests or gifts contingent upon certain events. Trusts are extremely flexible. So the clients signed the trust document containing all their plans for the management of assets for their heirs, left the document original with the attorney, and after their deaths, the named trustees would take over the trust management. Except then they had to put the pour-over will through probate.

The attorney, through neglect, intention, or ignorance, failed to "fund" the trust. At the death of the client the trust owned nothing. The assets were not transferred to the trust until after the probate process on the pour-over will was completed. Funding means to transfer assets, by deed, title transfer, or beneficiary designation, to the trust while the clients are still alive. Then, at death, there is nothing in the clients' names to probate. Everything would already be in the name of the trust, which can then immediately take effect under the control of the named trustees with no court involvement or cost at all. The clients' wishes were ultimately followed, but with much more complication and cost than necessary.

A pour-over will (see Appendix F) looks like a regular will, except it says in its dispositive clause that at the death of the will maker (testator), all the assets are to be transferred—or poured over—into the living trust. Most estate planning attorneys will create the trust and the pour-over will but intend to use the will only as a fail-safe document to ensure that any assets that were mistakenly not funded would ultimately find their way into the trust, albeit at the cost of probating that forgotten asset. We do not rely on the pour-over will to fund the trust. It is strictly a backup document we hope to never use. In this case, proper funding would have left nothing outside the trust to run through probate.

Keep in mind that it is the responsibility of the client to be sure to keep the trust funded and of the attorney to try to get everything into the trust initially. Buying a new home or property or getting new insurance or investments requires that the new asset be funded to the trust. If you do not do this, you are responsible for making your estate go through the probate process.

HOW TO AVOID PROBATE BY USING DEEDS: THE LADYBIRD DEED

If the only major asset of an estate is real estate, there are a few states (Florida, Michigan, West Virginia, Texas, and Vermont) that allow the use of a special type of deed to transfer property at death with no probate court involvement or permission. This so-called "ladybird deed," also known as an enhanced life estate deed, allows a person (the grantor) to transfer the property to others (grantees) at the grantor's death while retaining the owner's ability to sell, mortgage, or gift the property during his or her lifetime without the signatures or permission of the grantees. At the death of the grantor, the property automatically becomes the property of the named heirs on the deed.

Should the grantor decide to dispose of the property, mortgage it, or give it to someone else, he or she does not need the permission of the grantees to do so, since they have only a revocable contingent interest in the property.

This deed also has advantageous tax benefits. Since the gift to the grantees is a contingent gift, it is not complete until the grantor dies and the deed is still in effect. So, the tax basis for purposes of determining federal capital gains tax is the value as of the date of death, not the value at the time of the deed. That means there is no gain if the heirs sell right away.

A more modern type of deed that is used to avoid probate is called the transfer on death (TOD) deed. At last count, twenty-four states recognize this type of transfer. The TOD deed is very similar to the ladybird deed in that the grantor retains control of the property during his lifetime and can revoke the deed and mortgage, sell, or transfer the property. However, in most states that recognize the TOD, it has to be registered or filed with the recorder of deeds before the grantor's death, unlike the ladybird deed, which can be filed either before or after death, depending upon state law.

Using one of these types of deeds allows for immediate transfer of the real estate to the named heirs merely by filing the grantor's death certificate with the register of deeds where the property is located.

In states that do not allow a ladybird deed or a TOD, a deed can still be made in which the grantor retains the right to possession of the property during their lifetime with the title transferring automatically to the remaindermen at death. However, the grantor cannot sell, gift, or mortgage the property without the permission of the co-owners (and their spouses in most cases). While the interests of the remaindermen cannot be changed, the deed can be written in such a way that if a remainderman dies before the grantor, the share of that remainderman lapses and goes to the other remaindermen, if any, and if none, back to the grantor.

Other types of deeds that avoid probate include transfer from the property owner to others in the following ways. Keep in mind that making such a transfer could trigger a reassessment of the property's value for tax purposes, depending upon your local law. Check with your local tax assessor.

1. **Tenants in common.** This type of ownership allows two or more grantees to own the property jointly in independent shares, with no right of survivorship. The individual owners own their separate share of the property and can gift, sell, mortgage (in most cases), and leave it in a will to their own heirs. Once the property share is deeded to them, they do not need the permission of the other owners to manage their ownership shares. At the death of a tenant in common owner, his or her share is part of his or her estate and can pass under a will or trust. The grantor cannot revoke this ownership interest, as it is a completed legal transfer as soon as the deed is made and delivered.

2. **Joint tenancy with right of survivorship.** In this kind of ownership, the property belongs to two or more people jointly and their shares may not be transferred or sold without the consent of all the other owners (and their spouses in most cases). At the death of a joint tenant, that share lapses and automatically belongs to the surviving joint tenants pro rata. This is sometimes referred to as the "last man standing" rule. It is a popular scenario in British mysteries.

3. **Tenancy by the entireties.** This is co-ownership by a married couple. Transfer of the property requires the consent of both of them. Should one die before the other, the entire property automatically belongs to the survivor by merely filing the death certificate with the recorder of deeds.

Example

Be careful what kind of deed you are making, since the wrong choice and changed circumstances can lead to an unwanted end result. I once had a situation with an unmarried father with three adult children who made a deed to his kids for the family home. He had downloaded the deed form from an online legal form site. All three were married but the deed just named the three children, not the spouses, as tenants in common. No mention was made of the word "survivorship."

Then one of the children died, leaving a surviving wife, Dad's daughter-in-law. She contacted a lawyer, who informed the father that the wife wanted to partition the property or be paid her share of its value. Apparently, she was not so fond of her father-in-law once her husband was gone. Now, this was the father's only home, he was still alive, and he had assumed that the property would pass to his children only at his death.

The deed was intended as a probate-avoiding gift, but legally it was not doing what he had planned. The law was on her side. There was no right of survivorship. We had to go to court in an attempt to invalidate the deed on the basis of mistake, but in the end had to settle with the daughter-in-law to keep him in the home. Be careful doing your own legal work, even a simple deed, since unforeseen consequences can occur.

Transferring the property into the name of a revocable trust can accomplish the same thing as a deed, but it requires the drafting of a trust, which will be more costly than merely preparing a deed. I do not recommend that anyone draft their own deed, hoping to meet the statutory requirements for a probate-free title transfer. Hiring a local real estate attorney for services limited to only the deed preparation is the best way to be sure your intentions are carried out. If you don't have an attorney, a local title insurance company can either prepare the correct deed for you or refer you to a real estate attorney.

What if you own property in more than one state? Unless you have used a probate-avoiding technique for the property, you will have to go through some type of probate in every one of those states. The full probate would be in your home state with so-called ancillary probate in the other states. You can understand how this could greatly magnify your probate costs, since a separate attorney and a separate probate process would be required for each state. Using a trust or probate-avoiding deeds will eliminate probate everywhere.

AVOIDING PROBATE USING BENEFICIARY DESIGNATIONS

Beneficiaries can be used for a lot more than just life insurance. The only time life insurance ends up in your probated estate is if there is no named beneficiary, all beneficiaries died before you, or you named your estate as your beneficiary.

Your trust can be your life insurance beneficiary if you want the insurance payout to be distributed in the same way as all your other assets. Or you can name one or more individuals or institutions as beneficiaries. This does not have to be in equal shares. For example, you could do it in percentages, with different percentages for each beneficiary, all totaling 100 percent. Your church or a charity could be named for a percentage. So long as beneficiaries are named for the entire insurance payout, no probate is needed. Remain aware of what you have done. If a named beneficiary dies before you, depending upon the terms of the policy and state law, you might be leaving the deceased beneficiary's share to his or her estate, which means probate. If you divorce, remember to change your beneficiaries to avoid complications with the ex.

Also, you do not want to name minor children as beneficiaries because the court will, except where the dollar amount is small, appoint a conservator for them to manage the money until they are of age, and that conservator is likely to charge fees for that service. It is far better to name a probate-free trust as the beneficiary and have those funds added to other inheritances for the children and managed in the same way, even beyond the age of majority.

If your probate-avoiding plan involves beneficiary designations, any people objecting to the named beneficiary receiving anything will have a tough time, since these can be very difficult to challenge, unlike a will.

If you want a disabled person who is receiving governmental assistance to benefit from insurance funds, do not name them as a beneficiary even if they are of age. Government programs such as Medicaid usually are need-based. If a recipient inherits money, they could be disqualified from their benefits until the money is spent down, and thus would in fact receive no benefit from the money left to them.

Rather, leave the money to a properly drafted discretionary trust that will avoid disqualification, yet allow the recipient to get benefits from the fund. Alternatively, you could leave the money to someone else, a sibling perhaps, with the understanding that they will use it to benefit the disabled person. While this understanding might not be legally enforceable, in most cases it will be a safe arrangement.

Life insurance policies can also have a structured installment payment beneficiary designation. In the event you have a beneficiary who is likely to waste a lump sum insurance payout, leaving the insurance to them with instructions that it be spread out in annual payments over a period of years ensures that they will have a guaranteed income during that time. A bonus is that life insurance benefits are not taxable income. Some insurance companies will even reduce the policy premiums if the installment payout plan is selected.

PAY-ON-DEATH (POD) AND TRANSFER-ON-DEATH (TOD) ACCOUNTS

Similar to beneficiary designations, these allow the owner of certain accounts to direct who will inherit the asset on death without resorting to probate. TODs are typically for investment or retirement accounts, while PODs are for bank accounts such as savings, CDs, and money market accounts. While the person named as the transferee can take the asset directly, it is also possible to name a trust as the beneficiary so that the asset is added to the trust principal. If the assets transferred are investments that have appreciated, the new owner receives a stepped-up tax basis and should not have to pay capital gains tax on the appreciation in value. (Be sure to check all current tax rules on anything mentioned in this book, since tax and other laws change frequently and I am not allowed to give tax advice in this book.)

Some institutions and states will not allow a bank account to be titled in the name of a trust, so a POD designation is the alternative. Account types might also allow a beneficiary, which is effectively the same thing.

To create one of these designations, the bank or other institution will have a fill-in-the-blank form for you. This can be changed at any time. To collect, the designee merely has to show identification and provide a copy of the death certificate.

Do not just put someone else's name on your investment or deposit accounts as a co-owner. Doing so not only means that they now can access the accounts for their own use, but also that the account might be subject to the new co-owner's debts, lawsuits, garnishments, taxes, or student loans. Be safe, not sorry.

GIFTS

Probate only applies to assets left in the name of a person who has died. If that asset is given away before death, it is obviously not probatable since it was no longer in that person's name. Certain assets have title certificates or some document stating the name of the owner, so those take care of identifying who owns that asset. The importance of identifying the making of a gift is to avoid not only probate of that item but also elimination of confusion among competing heirs-at-law.

Automobiles, boats, trailers, motorcycles, and the like have titles or registrations, so if you transfer title to another person the making of a gift is pretty clear-cut. Some states even allow "and/or" titles so that you can title your car in a name such as "John Doe or James Doe." Then the vehicle belongs to whoever lives the longest, and either owner can sell it without the consent of the other. Other states will allow joint titles such as "John Doe and James Doe JWROS" (joint with right of survivorship).

Autos can also carry a TOD on the title itself in seventeen states. While any loans on the car would still have to be paid (typically in cash at the death of the borrower), no probate would be needed to transfer the title. The owner can change her mind at any time and either eliminate the TOD designation or change it to another person. But be sure to check with your auto insurance carrier if you change the title in any way to avoid problems in the event of an insurance claim.

There are even specific state laws that allow an automatic transfer of title to a vehicle or boat just by filing a form with the court and paying a small fee, if there is no probate case open and the value of all such vehicles is less than a state-mandated maximum.

Non-titled assets such as furniture, jewelry, collections, artworks and so forth, if valuable and/or subject to possible dispute among relatives, can be assigned to your trust, if any, or you can merely make out a list of the assets, whom you gave them to, and sign and date it. You should state that while you are making this gift immediately, you reserve the right to retain possession of it during your lifetime. Be sure the list will not be found or destroyed by any heir who might not agree with your decisions. Often family heirloom items are of greater interest to an heir than the money they might receive.

I have had lawsuits over purported gifts where the intention of the giver was unclear. In one case it was an antique billiard table—the deceased had said one of her daughters was to get it, but the other daughter, who had been storing it, said it was a gift. The daughter who had it ended up paying the other daughter half the value. The attorney fees to fight about the table were probably five times the value of the table, but neither side would give in.

In community property states, you should check with your lawyer to see if both spouses have to agree to a gift. If such consent is required and not gotten, the courts can overturn the intended gift.

The Gift Tax

If a gift is less than the taxable threshold for gift taxes, it passes to the person receiving it without any tax consequence. There is also no income tax on a gift, since it is not income. The annual gift tax exclusion amount for 2019 is $15,000 per donee, and there is no limit to the number of donees. Thus, a donor can give as many $15,000 gifts to as many people as desired with no upper limit, and a married couple has two exclusion amounts available annually. A married couple with four married children could gift $240,000 each year to their children and their spouses and still stay within the annual exclusion amount and would incur no gift tax.

But what if a person has a great deal of money that he wants to give away? The gift tax laws (as of 2019) allow a lifetime exclusion amount of $11,400,000, which is in addition to the annual exclusion amount. For a couple, this would be $22,800,000. With a properly timed gift there would be no probate, no income tax, and no gift tax. The gift does not have to be just cash. It could be investments, family businesses, real estate, or any other assets. Capital gains tax may or may not be an issue if the gift is structured properly to take advantage of a stepped-up tax basis in the property being transferred.

Most of us aren't going to approach these maximums, but it's enough to know that gifting will work in the right situations. There's the lottery, right? Reducing the size of your probatable estate with gifts is a great tool, provided that there are enough assets left for the donor's needs.

CHAPTER THREE

Using Trusts as a Probate-Avoiding Tool

The popularity of living trusts has spread to the point that now many states, most notably California, have promulgated laws recognizing and regulating trusts. There is a model Uniform Trust Code[1] that has been adopted in different forms by more than thirty states. This recognition of trusts as a valid and effective estate planning device is long overdue. It seems attorneys have decided to join the trust revolution rather than fight it, and now many call themselves trust specialists where such a specialty is authorized. Trusts are becoming the preferred method for attorneys and clients to settle estates and avoid the probate process.

Having said that, I have spent a great deal of time reviewing trusts prepared by other attorneys at the request of new clients and find serious problems with many of them. There are templates and fill-in-the-blank programs that are available to attorneys who need to prepare a trust. They don't just make up these documents off the top of their heads. Unfortunately for the clients, some of these boilerplate programs are completely inappropriate for the needs of a client or are legally out of date.

In years past, trusts were considered by many estate planners as primarily a device to minimize or eliminate estate

---

1 "Trust Code," Uniform Law Commission, last modified June 21, 2019, https://www.uniformlaws.org/committees/community-home?communitykey =193ff839-7955-4846-8f3c-ce74ac23938d&tab=groupdetails.

taxes. The general public thought that trusts, if they thought about them at all, were for rich people. Taxes were a serious concern back in 1997, when estates in excess of $600,000 were taxed at a 55 percent rate. With a house, savings, and life insurance, there were lots of people who could have been subject to the tax. The threshold has gradually increased, until by 2019 the estate must exceed $11,400,000 before there is any tax. Estate tax avoidance is no longer an issue for most of us. Of course, laws change, but the estate tax is more likely to be eliminated entirely rather than go back to the old tax rates. We shall see.

The problem with using a trust to avoid taxes is twofold. First, couples who once might have been subject to estate taxes had complex tax-avoidance trusts prepared that placed serious restrictions on a surviving spouse's access to the marital assets. At the death of one spouse, the trust would be split into two or more new trusts with different rules for management and dispersion of the assets in each. This required more legal as well as accounting services, both at a high cost. Discussion of A/B trusts, marital trusts, credit-shelter trusts, bypass trusts, and QTIP trusts are beyond the scope of this book, but suffice it to say that they are only necessary for very large estates, and those folks are not reading this book. Since most of these estates are no longer exposed to potential federal estate taxes, these kinds of trusts complicate the settlement process and create problems for the heirs. It can be a simple matter to amend the trusts to simplify them, but this is rarely done.

Second, these complex and outdated trusts are still being used when they are no longer needed or appropriate. One justification some attorneys rely upon is that the rules change all the time and it might be that the exemption amount will decrease, making more estates subject to taxation. History does not agree. The exemption amount has increased steadily over the last twenty years, and there is legislation introduced annually to eliminate federal estate taxes completely. However, all I can say is, rely on the advice of your lawyers but get a second opinion. Also, a state inheritance tax exists in some states that might require some planning to minimize or avoid.

Avoiding probate is the focus of this book. Trusts are the best way for anything except the simplest estates, but in most cases, there is no need for a complex trust provided that the trust contains all the necessary and appropriate provisions to cover potential issues.

Trusts are far and away the most simple and effective way to avoid probate and protect your assets for the benefit of your heirs. I have explained why probate should be avoided due to its cost, time delays, and lack of privacy. But what is this trust thing that I am encouraging people to use?

Trusts are not a new idea. In English and Muslim law, they date back to the eleventh century, the time of the Crusades. When the knights went to the East, they turned the ownership of their estates over to a trustee who was to manage them for the years while the knight was away. The understanding was that the trustee would return the lands to the knight when he returned. But sometimes the trustee refused. The courts took up the matter and determined that while legal ownership was in the name of the trustee, beneficial ownership remained with the knight, hence the name: beneficiary.

By the nineteenth and twentieth centuries, trusts were a business artifice used to control ownership in multiple businesses and create monopolies as well as a way for the wealthy to pass on their estates through multiple generations. Legal restrictions were put on these types of trusts to limit how long such a trust arrangement could continue, so that when the trust ended it could be taxed. When you hear that trusts are just for the wealthy, remember that while there used to be some truth to that, it is no longer true.

By far, the number-one recommended method for avoiding probate is the revocable living trust. Way back in 1965, Norman F. Dacey, who was not a lawyer, created a legal uproar by advocating probate avoidance using a living trust. The trouble started when he provided forms allowing people to create their own.

He was charged with the unauthorized practice of law, a criminal charge, of which he was convicted in Connecticut and was also sued by the New York Lawyers Association. He ultimately beat the New York case on appeal and the resulting publicity resulted in the sale of over two million books on how to avoid probate. The entrenched probate lawyers and bar associations did all they could to stop him, but the ball had started rolling.

Estate tax avoidance became a primary purpose of trusts when the tax rates soared from 50 to 70 percent on some estates. Attorneys earned their fees when such a big tax bite could be lessened. Nowadays there are still a few people who have to plan around these taxes, but for most of us the trust has assumed a new purpose, which is management of inheritances for beneficiaries who can't or shouldn't manage the money themselves, and for avoidance of probate, which is the subject of this book.

However, clients don't come to see me because they are hoping to avoid probate, and they don't usually ask for a trust.

Most often they come to me to have their will made. Because that's what responsible people do, right? During the initial interview I ask them what they want to see happen to their assets at their deaths. If it's a married couple with children, the typical answer is that they want everything to go to each other and at both deaths to have everything go to their children equally.

At that point, I explain that they do not need a will and that any attorney preparing a will with those terms is doing them a disservice. As we now know, a will does not avoid probate, and if a couple in their situation dies, what they are asking for in a will is exactly what would happen if they had no will at all. The will would be probated and the procedure would be just the same as it would be if there were no will. Same cost, same time delays, same end result.

Then I ask other questions. Are your children good money managers? Are any of them disabled or receiving any governmental assistance? How old are they? If there are minor children, have you chosen a guardian for them in the event both of you die while they are still minors? Would you want your children to receive their inheritance in a lump sum at your deaths or instead have it spread out over time? Do you plan on making any charitable gifts at death? Are there grandchildren? Do you own a family business? How about vacation property or real estate in another state? Do you have parents alive? How much life insurance do you have? Is this a second marriage for either of you? Were there children before or outside of the current marriage? Do you have a premarital agreement? Who do you see being in charge of winding up your affairs at your deaths? Who would make medical and business decisions for you if you become mentally incapacitated?

The answers to these questions will determine the type of trust I would recommend and will solve the other serious problems that might arise aside from just avoiding probate. If they still want a will after knowing all about trusts, then I would make one for them, but reluctantly.

REVOCABLE TRUSTS VERSUS IRREVOCABLE TRUSTS

First, some definitions:

- The person making the trust, the trust owner, is called the *grantor*.
- The person in charge of managing and/or distributing a trust is called the *trustee*.
- While the grantor is alive and competent, she can be both the grantor and the trustee. At her death, another person or persons take over to carry out the terms of the trust. These are called *successor trustees*.
- Those who are given the trust assets as set out in the trust agreement are the *trust beneficiaries*. The grantor can also be a trust beneficiary during her lifetime.

Revocable means that the trust is changeable by the grantor. People don't often revoke their trust but do amend them as circumstances change. If the trust is irrevocable, it usually can be neither revoked nor amended. We do use irrevocable trusts in certain situations, which will be described later.

A *living trust* (sometimes called an *inter vivos trust*) just refers to the fact that the trust comes into existence while the trust grantor is alive, rather than coming into existence at her death. A *testamentary trust*—one contained within the provisions of a will—is not a living trust, since it does not come into existence until the grantor's death. A trust, when signed, is something like a business. Example: The Doe Bakery Corporation is a business and can have multiple bank accounts in its own name. It can own the bakery building, the delivery van, the equipment and supplies, even the doughnuts belonging to the business. But Mr. and Mrs. Doe own the Doe Bakery. The business, as a corporation, has a set of bylaws, which are rules governing how the business operates. If the owners die, the business is still alive and likely still making doughnuts under new management.

A trust is like that in many ways. Your trust can own your real estate, bank accounts, investments, vehicles, personal property and furniture, and can be the beneficiary of insurance and accounts, but you own the trust. So long as you are alive and competent, you can revoke the trust, change its terms, and spend its assets. The trust has instructions that determine how changes can be made, the powers trustees have in relation to borrowing against or buying and selling assets, and what happens if you, the trust grantor, become disabled or die. It can continue in existence after your death to provide management of assets for your heirs. It is very important that all the appropriate language be in the trust document to most effectively carry out your wishes.

A trust, as a legal entity, actually needs a name so that assets can be transferred into and out of the name of the trust. Investment accounts will be under the name of the trust and it can have its own federal tax employer identification number rather than using the grantor's Social Security number. It might be called any of these names:

- The John Doe and Jane Doe Revocable Living Trust
- The John Doe and Jane Doe Trust
- The Doe Family Trust
- The John and Jane Doe Loving Trust
- Bob (LOL—the point being that the trust can be called anything)

Since some of us have more than one trust, it helps to identify the particular trust by adding the date the trust was created to its name. This is usually formatted as follows: "The John Doe Trust under agreement dated April 1, 2021" *or* foreshortened as "U/A 1st April 2021."

As explained earlier, a trust is like a will in that it is a written document saying who gets what at the death of the grantor, who is in charge of seeing that this happens, and directs when the grantees receive their inheritances after the grantor dies. But unlike a will, trust assets do not have to go through the probate process in order to distribute the estate assets, and no court is required to be involved in the trust management or distribution to trust beneficiaries. A trust is also a legal entity—in other words, a legal person, which has the ability to own things just like a real person.

After the trust is written and signed, it is born into existence and then needs to be funded. As described earlier, *funded* means that assets are put into the name of the trust in one way or another. It can be directly, by deed or title transfer, or planned for the future by listing the trust as the beneficiary or by transfer-on-death or pay-on-death designations. Insurance policies, real estate, vehicles, bank and investment accounts, business interests, personal property, collections—essentially everything a grantor owns can be transferred into the name of his trust. When you die the trust already owns your stuff, so there remains nothing left in your individual name to probate. The trust says what happens to the things it owns, and the trustee sees that those directions are followed.

While a grantor is alive and competent, there are no restrictions on what she can do with the assets in a revocable trust. Assets can be bought, sold, mortgaged, destroyed, or given away at the whim of the grantor. There is no real downside.

At the grantor's disability—typically mental or physical incompetency, as determined by two physicians and as instructed in her power of attorney and in the trust itself—the trust becomes irrevocable and the successor trustee takes over and uses the assets for the grantor's benefit. At her death, the trustee follows the instructions as to distributing the remaining trust assets to the final beneficiaries.

Probate avoidance is a major advantage of the trust due to its savings of time, complexity, and money, but for many grantors the asset management features are even more important. Sometimes it is necessary to structure an inheritance to be certain that the inherited assets are preserved and used for the beneficiary's benefit. Here are common examples.

CHILDREN AS HEIRS

If you leave your estate in a typical manner, it might say everything goes to your spouse, and if he is already deceased then it all goes to your children equally. That's a commonsense and normal intention, but it has several potential problems.

First, of course, is what if the children are minors? They can't do most of the transactional tasks needed to manage money, pay taxes, and do banking and investments. If you say nothing else other than that they inherit your estate, then their inheritance would be turned over to a court-appointed conservator to hold and manage for them until they reach the age of majority. That brings the court into play with its attendant costs and hindrances.

Then, should the money be turned over to them when they turn eighteen? While some teenagers would be able to handle their own financial affairs, most would not. A young person might consider themselves rich, even with not so many thousands of dollars—therefore, why go to college? Friends will be influencing them and soon the money could be gone. No cash and no education.

Parents generally like the idea of having a child's inheritance managed by someone else, a trustee for instance, who will then use the money for the child's education and other needs, distributing it either at a given age or spread out in incremental distributions. For minors, the instruction might be that the trust fund can be used for educational expenses, then one-third upon graduation or reaching age twenty-five, whichever comes first, then half of the remainder at age thirty and the balance at age thirty-five. This kind of plan encourages getting an education. The thinking could be as follows: *I can go get a low-paying unskilled job until I am twenty-five, or go to college and have it paid for by the trust.* Which sounds better?

As to the next two installments, it gives the child time to reflect on his mistakes if he blew the first installment on bad decisions, investments, or relationships. Then there are the children who are their own worst enemies, even when grown. There is just no way they can be given any lump sum without wasting it. So, a trust can be structured for that child to provide a lifetime income. This could be an instruction that a lifetime annuity be purchased with the trust fund money or that the trustee use the funds to pay for the beneficiary's income and expenses over a period of time.

I generally suggest a clause in the trust that does not allow a beneficiary to "anticipate" his inheritance. This means that he cannot sell, borrow against, or assign his right to receive money. This is to avoid companies that will buy out an expected inheritance for a lump sum, which is typically far less than what the beneficiary would receive over time and thus make an end run around the plan that you set up.

Another potential problem is when you name the trustee of the child's funds to be the same person as the child's guardian. This is a potential conflict of interest. I represented some children who inherited when they were in their early teens. They lived with the guardian and the guardian used their money to help support them, but also used it for her own children's expenses and benefit. New appliances and furniture for her house also came from the children's trust fund, as did a swimming pool. While the children all enjoyed the use of these things, the things stayed with the guardian after the children were of age. This and other expenses charged to the trust left little to the children when it came time to close down the trust.

We sued, but the trustee/guardian had already spent the money and there was no way she was going to be able to repay them. This situation could easily have been avoided by appointing a separate trustee from the guardian or having co-trustees or, even better, having a trust protector as described later in this book. It was a badly drafted trust, and this is one case where probate court supervision could have prevented the misuse of funds. Sometimes a poorly made trust is worse than having to go through probate.

SPECIAL-NEEDS TRUSTS

Medical coverage is often more important to a beneficiary than a monetary inheritance. Lots of people rely upon Medicaid or other need-based programs to pay for their chronic medical expenses. If they should inherit an unrestricted amount of money, they could be disqualified from receiving their benefits until the money has been exhausted. So, they receive no actual benefit from the inheritance, it being required to be used for their medical care. Probate court conservatorships cannot help in this situation.

A trust can include provisions that the share of that person is to be held in a discretionary trust, which gives the beneficiary no right to these assets without the permission of the trustee, and at the death of the beneficiary any remaining assets would go to one or more other named beneficiaries, the so-called remaindermen. The trustee could use some of the money—less than what would disqualify the beneficiary from the program—for the benefit of the beneficiary but would not be required to do so. Paying for a vacation at a theme park, for example, or buying toys, games, and clothing would likely not disqualify the beneficiary. This type of discretionary Medicaid trust takes careful drafting by an experienced trust attorney, since the law changes often in these areas and varies from state to state. It is a personal decision to do it this way, since some would think it a way of taking unfair advantage of the Medicaid program. (I have never had anyone say no to this suggested approach.)

JOINT OR SINGLE TRUSTS

Trusts can be joint or individual. Married couples typically opt for joint trusts, although they can have individual ones if they choose. Couples who are in second marriages, where each brought assets into the marriage and might have children from prior relationships, often have a desire to use the assets of the first to die to benefit the survivor, with the residue going to that person's separate children at both their deaths. The trust of the first to die usually becomes irrevocable at that time. As we know, that means it cannot be changed. The trust has to be carefully written to protect the survivor as well as the children. The surviving spouse is normally not a sole trustee.

Even in relatively modest family estates, an irrevocable survivor's trust is sometimes used. It often happens that one of the parties already had a house into which the new spouse moved. The house-owning spouse will give the survivor the irrevocable right to live in the house as a primary residence for life, with the house going to the children at both deaths. Be sure, though, that if this type of trust is created it also protects the survivor's right to the use of the household furnishings and possibly automobile. I had a case where the children of the deceased parent actually removed all the furniture, right down to the kitchen dishes and silverware, even though they could not get possession of the house itself. People can be real jerks when a stepparent dies, and it often comes as a tragic surprise to the survivor. A trust can be written to provide for the individual wants and needs of nearly any family situation.

A grantor does not have to be married to create a joint trust. I have prepared joint trusts for a parent and child and many for unmarried couples.

As you can see, the flexibility of revocable trusts, both joint and single, allows you to accomplish your testamentary goals while avoiding the high cost and time consumption of the probate process. The vast range of trust types and provisions is why, in my opinion, preprinted or online trust forms are not suitable for most people and can lead to unintended outcomes if not carefully drafted.

DISCRETIONARY TRUSTS

Irrevocable trusts are often used in gifting situations. You can set aside money to be held in trust for someone, to be distributed according to your instructions and under the control and management of a trustee other than yourself. This might be a trust for grandchildren, which you can add to from time to time with the parents as trustees. It could be used for educational expenses or distributed in installments as you direct. Or it could be a total discretionary trust where the trustees have total say-so as to when, if, and what amount should be used for the beneficiaries. If the beneficiary dies or disclaims the trust funds, you would direct who would get the remaining funds in the trust. These irrevocable trusts would remove the funds from your probatable and taxable estate. You can also set up trusts to care for pets or for charitable purposes.

ASSET PROTECTION TRUSTS

I mention these because they get a lot of press, though not just for probate avoidance. The asset protection trust pitch is that you can create a trust, usually with a legal home base in another country, put your assets in it, and even open bank accounts with debit cards in the trust name. If you are sued or subject to high tax rates where you actually live, the trusts protect you from having your funds taken by creditors, bankruptcy, lawsuits, and divorce judgments. While most of these are legal plans, they have significant downsides and can be pricey.

The basic idea is to create an irrevocable discretionary trust with someone besides yourself as the trustee. You can only get at your trust funds if the trustee agrees, and only under limited circumstances. If you can't get them, neither can anyone else. Typically, the plans also include creating a limited liability company (LLC) to manage the assets and to hold title to some of them to hide the actual ownership. You own the LLC, which sets up the trust, and you decide who becomes the trustee. It is a rich person's way of hiding money and can be used for money laundering.

Problems can arise and often do if you try to create this kind of trust after the trouble you are trying to avoid has already begun. There are criminal laws that apply if it can be shown that you fraudulently divested yourself of assets in order to avoid creditors. These are usually called fraudulent conveyance statutes. Similarly, a divorce or bankruptcy court may be able to set aside any such transfer if it was made too closely in time to the bankruptcy or divorce.

COMPLEX TAX-SAVING TRUSTS

What if your trust was set up years ago, based on tax laws at that time, and was intended to avoid estate taxes? Because of the changes in estate tax laws discussed earlier, it is unlikely that you would ever have to be concerned about taxation. The existing trust, which is likely filled with complicated formulas for splitting the trust at the death of one partner, creating a marital trust and a bypass trust, can now be simplified. This will eliminate accounting and attorney fees at the death of one and again at the death of the other to settle the complex trust. While this type of trust was appropriate and necessary when the tax threshold was low, it is likely not needed any longer.

For much of the last thirty years, the estate tax threshold has been increasing so that fewer estates are now taxable. The threshold is the amount your estate can have in it without being taxed by the IRS. The taxable estate is not the same as the probate estate. All assets, including those in trusts and those like life insurance that pass by beneficiary designation, are counted as taxable assets for estate tax purposes. By the time you add up the values of insurance, retirement and investment accounts, real estate, personal property, intangibles, and other assets, many people—not just the rich—were subject to estate taxes. And the tax rates were high—up to 45 percent of the amount over the threshold. Having trusts could easily double the amount of exemption for a married couple, so we made a lot of tax-saving trusts back then.

One of insurance agents' favorite plans to push used to be irrevocable life insurance trusts, set up to create a fund to pay the massive estate taxes. This cost the client money for both the trust and the life insurance, but presumably saved money in the long run. If you have one of these and are substantially below the exemption amount, you probably don't need either the trust or the insurance policy any longer. Ask your lawyer. It could be appropriate to defund the existing trust and replace it with a simpler and easier-to-understand version.

A simple trust, such as the example in Appendix E, is pretty easy to understand, but in fact I can make a perfectly legal trust in just two or three pages for simple estate plans. More pages do not make a better trust. I have seen trusts running upwards of a hundred pages for seemingly ordinary family situations. They are mostly boilerplate. To repeat my warnings: whatever you do, be sure to run it past your lawyer before you commit to anything, and always get a second unbiased opinion.

Here's a chart illustrating the changes in the estate tax exemptions. Keep in mind it is likely to continue to change in the future. It may even decrease. The tax rate applies only to the amount in excess of the estate tax exemption amount.

Year	Estate Tax Exemption	Top Estate Tax Rate
1997	$600,000	55%
1998	$625,000	55%
1999	$650,000	55%
2000	$675,000	55%
2001	$675,000	55%
2002	$1,000,000	50%
2003	$1,000,000	49%
2004	$1,500,000	48%
2005	$1,500,000	47%
2006	$2,000,000	46%
2007	$2,000,000	45%
2008	$2,000,000	45%
2009	$3,500,000	45%
2010	$5,000,000	35%
2011	$5,000,000	35%
2012	$5,120,000	35%
2013	$5,250,000	40%
2014	$5,340,000	40%
2015	$5,430,000	40%
2016	$5,450,000	40%
2017	$5,490,000	40%
2018	$5,490,000	40%
2019	$11,400,000	40%

REVOKING AN EXISTING TRUST

When we say revocable, we usually mean changeable. But revoke also means revoke. If your circumstances change and there are simpler ways to leave your estate free of probate as described in chapter 2, your trust can be revoked so you can use the alternate methods. Or it might be that there has been a divorce or disagreement between the owners of a joint trust and it has to be revoked. How do you do that? Unless your trust has been filed with a probate court, you do not need to sign any special form to revoke it. I know there are lawyers out there who will prepare such a form, but is it not necessary.

The simplest way is to remove all the assets from the trust name and put them back in your own name. If there are unrecorded deeds you signed to transfer your real estate to the trust, merely destroy them and the property stays in its original ownership. If the deed to the trust has been recorded, make a new deed from the trust back to you or in an ownership type as described in chapter 2.

Beneficiary designations can be changed so that the trust is not the beneficiary; the same with TOD and POD accounts. Titles to vehicles and boats can be returned to your name. The personal property assignment form can be destroyed as well, and a will can be made that automatically rescinds the pour-over will.

The goal is "repeal and replace." Be sure no assets are left in the trust name and that none will flow to the trust at your death. If the trust owns nothing now or in the future, it is a non-entity. You must then set up your non-trust probate-avoiding plan by way of deeds, beneficiary designations, joint ownership, or TOD and POD designations.

UNDERSTANDING THE TRUST

A properly written trust can be lengthy, and depending upon the intentions of the grantors and the composition of their assets, it may seem complicated to a non-lawyer. However, by structuring it much like a book, it can be much easier to understand. Searching for important provisions is also easier if it is properly set up. I like the textbook approach with a table of contents. This should be the very first page of the trust, so that frequently asked questions are easily answered. You can use this format and fill it out yourself if your attorney doesn't do it this way.

Here is a sample for the John H. Doe Trust.

Summary of Trust Provisions

Grantor Name: John H. Doe, an unmarried man
Grantor Residence Address at Time of Signing: 1234 Elm Street, Anytown, Michigan
State Law Governing the Trust (Situs): Michigan
Name of Trust: The John H. Doe Revocable Trust dated April 1, 2021
Date Signed: April 1, 2021
Initial Trustee: John H. Doe
Name of Successor Trustee on Death or Disability of Grantor: Kevin I. Doe
  Address: 1221 North Main Street, Detroit, MI
Alternate Successor Trustee: Judith Doe-Jones
  Address: 1900 Happy Valley, San Diego, CA

Powers of Grantor as Trustee
  Section 6 Page _____, et seq
Powers of Successor Trustee at disability of Grantor
  Section 7 Page _____, et seq
Powers of Successor Trustee at death of Grantor
  Section 7 Page _____, et seq
Distribution of Trust assets at death of Grantor
  Section 8 Page _____, et seq
Distribution of personal property at death of Grantor
  Appendix 1 Page _____
Amendments to Trust
  Appendix 2 Page _____
List of personal property to be distributed and to whom

Note that this summary is not a part of the trust document but merely a reference tool for accessing the document language.

NECESSARY DECISIONS BEFORE
MAKING YOUR TRUST

What your attorney should ask (see Appendix D):

1. **What are your assets?** Your attorney will need copies of all deeds, business ownership records, investments, life insurance policies, websites and online assets, collections, vehicle/boat/trailer titles or registrations, business equipment, patents/trademarks, royalties, personal property, leases, expected inheritances, ongoing lawsuits to which you are a party, foreign assets, or out-of-state assets. Providing these now will ensure that no assets are overlooked at your death that would otherwise have to be probated.

   At the death of one client, I was asked to assist in inventorying assets prior to an estate sale. I found a manila envelope tucked in among some books on the deceased's bookshelf. It contained a paid-up life insurance policy worth $250,000. No one knew about this, and if I hadn't found it, the policy could have gone unclaimed. It is a good idea to have a small personal safe in which you keep a summary of your assets. You might also include a list of owned domain names and passwords to websites and to unlock your computer and telephone to assist in locating assets at your death. You do not want the state to be your heir because no one knew about a particular account or item.

2. **What is your family history, i.e. children, marriages, parents, siblings?** Sometimes families become estranged, and whoever is handling your affairs might need to contact all the family members. Children born out of wedlock or from previous undisclosed marriages need to be identified so as to include or exclude them. I have had to hire private investigators to track down heirs whose location was unknown.

3. **Who will be in charge of your estate at your death (your trustee)?** Be sure to clear this with them since even if you appointed them, they are not required to do this job. Will this person be compensated? Alternates should also be named in the event the first choice is unable or unwilling to be in charge.

4. **Who will make medical decisions for you?** First and second choices should be named. Again, be sure to ask them if they will agree. In most states they will have to consent in writing.

5. **Who will handle your affairs at your disability (person with power of attorney)?** See Appendix C.

6. **How will your assets be distributed at your death (to whom and when)?** Do you want any restrictions placed on asset distributions?

7. **What if a named beneficiary of your assets dies before you (what happens to that share)?**

8. **Where do you keep lists of computer, telephone, and internet passwords and usernames?**

9. **Who do you want to take guardianship of your minor children?** Talk it over with them and have an alternate in mind as well.

A CHECKLIST OF SUGGESTED TRUST PROVISIONS

Here are some suggested provisions that should be in all trusts to make them work well for you. These might not be in the form books or in the trust prepared for you by your lawyer.

Keep in mind that these are suggested provisions, and the actual language used in the trust document should be written by your attorney in accordance with state law. Attorneys attend conferences and seminars on trusts and estate planning and are often given sample forms and language to use in legal documents of a shareware basis. This helps keep us all current with the law and practice. We use these or modify them to fit our needs, so after a while, it can be impossible to find who wrote the first version. So the following paragraphs might include some of these and are included to show how the suggested provisions might read.

Joint Trusts: Who Makes Decisions?

For joint trusts, specify who can make decisions on behalf of the trust. This includes trust asset management as well as amending or revoking the trust. There is a danger in allowing either of the grantors to act independently without the consent of the other. And you need to state whether the powers of the surviving grantor as trustee are limited in any way at the death or disability of the other grantor. Here are two examples:

1. Either grantor can act for the trust independent of the other.

Trustee Designation:

Husband and wife are hereby designated as Co-Trustees. The Co-Trustees may serve jointly or severally and either shall have full authority to act for the Trust independently. Should either husband or wife become unable because of death, incapacity, or other cause, to serve as a Co-Trustee, or should either resign as Co-Trustee before the natural termination of this Trust, the remaining Co-Trustee, husband or wife, shall thereafter serve as sole Trustee.

Amendment and Revocation:

Grantors hereby retain the following powers, exercisable at any time during their lifetimes:

1. To withdraw, sell, invest, transfer, or encumber any of the property included in the trust estate.
2. To amend the provisions of this trust declaration in any respect, without the necessity of securing the consent of the other grantor or trustee to such changes.
3. To revoke this trust.

Or,

2. Both grantors must participate in all trust transactions.

Trustee Designation:

Husband and wife are hereby designated as Co-Trustees. The Co-Trustees shall serve jointly and neither shall have full authority to act for the Trust independently. Should either husband or wife become unable because of death, incapacity, or other cause, to serve as a Co-Trustee, or should either resign as Co-Trustee before the natural termination of this Trust, the remaining Co-Trustee, husband or wife, shall thereafter serve as sole Trustee. Co-Trustees can agree to appoint by power of attorney the other trustee to act for him or her regarding specific actions or transactions of the trust.

Amendment and Revocation:

Grantors hereby retain the following joint powers, exercisable by their joint action at any time during their lifetimes:
1. To withdraw, sell, invest, transfer, or encumber any of the property included in the trust estate.
2. To amend the provisions of this trust declaration in any respect.
3. To revoke this trust.

Couples will often agree to allow either of them to act for the trust without the consent of the other. It does make management of assets, such as investing, check writing, taxes, and so forth, easier. As long as they act in good faith, this type of provision works fine. The problems come when they experience marital problems. One partner would have the ability to secretly transfer the trust assets without prior notification to his or her partner. Even knowing this, couples still often trust each other to have full authority over the trust assets.

Problems also occur at the death of one partner if the survivor decides to change the distribution provisions of the trust, especially if there are stepchildren involved. It is not uncommon to have a distribution plan that divides all trust assets equally among the children of both partners. When one dies, the survivor sometimes decides to amend the trust to favor his or her own children by either cutting out the partner's kids or reducing the shares going to them. That possibility is less likely if a provision such as this is added:

> *Amendment by a Surviving Grantor:*
> At the death or disability of one grantor before the other, the survivor shall continue to act as trustee and shall have the right to amend the trust, but shall not be able to amend it in such a way as to reduce the previous pro-rata monetary share of the children of the other grantor; nor shall the survivor have the power to remove assets from this trust ownership if such removal acts to effectively reduce the share to those children. This provision does not, however, affect the right of the survivor to use the trust assets for his or her own support and the beneficiaries shall have no right to supervise or approve any normal expenditure of the survivor, recognizing that the primary use of trust assets is for the benefit of the grantors during their lifetimes.

Successor Trustees

The grantor is usually the trustee—that is, the person who is in charge of the trust and its assets. But if the grantor becomes physically or mentally incapacitated or dies, someone has to take over the operation of the trust for the benefit of the grantor, or in case of the grantor's death, to carry out the grantor's instructions on management or distribution of the trust assets. The trust will become irrevocable at that point. As we know, irrevocable means unchangeable. So whatever terms were in the written trust at that point are the grantor's final word. The successor trustee should not have the legal authority to change the terms of the trust but merely carries out its existing terms.

Here is a sample of typical language in the trust to be sure that happens:

Revocation or Alteration by Grantor Alone:
The rights of revocation, withdrawal, alteration, and amendment may only be exercised by the Grantor or the surviving Grantor during the Grantor's lifetime, and may not be exercised by any other person, including an agent acting under a power of attorney, a guardian, or a conservator.

It is important that anyone reading the trust document understands what a successor trustee, or a person who is the grantor's power of attorney, can or cannot do. Sometimes those with a power of attorney (the agent or attorney-in-fact) think they have all the legal powers of the person giving them the power. Care must be taken that the agent's powers, spelled out in the power of attorney document, specifically limit the power and prohibit creating a will or amending or revoking a trust. Also, it is a bad idea to name different people for the role of successor trustee and agent under a power of attorney since that could create a conflict of powers over the same assets. See paragraph 17 in the sample power of attorney in Appendix C.

Appointment of Successor Trustees and Alternates

I strongly recommend that alternates be named as trustees in the event the trustee you named is unable or unwilling to act as such. As part of your own annual review, be certain that your choice is still appropriate. If you created your trust while your children were minors and could not act as trustees, but now they are of age and sufficiently competent to act as trustee, you need to amend your trust. If there is no named trustee available, the document should specify a procedure for selecting a trustee. Otherwise the trust may end up in front of a probate court judge so that a trustee can be legally appointed. You don't want that since it is typical for the judge to appoint a professional trustee at professional rates.

Trustees:

All Trustees are to serve without bond. Co-Trustees may divide their duties among themselves as they may agree. The following will act as Trustees of any Trusts created by this Trust Agreement, in the following order of succession:

First: The undersigned, Joseph Jones and Matilda Jones.

Second: The surviving spouse.

Third: At the death or incapacity of the surviving spouse, Timothy Jones and Linda Jones shall serve as Successor Co-Trustees.

Fourth: If either of them cannot act as Trustee, then the other shall serve as sole successor Trustee.

Last: If there is no Trustee named above who is able or willing to act as Trustee then a Trustee may be chosen by the majority of Beneficiaries, with a parent or legal guardian voting for minor Beneficiaries; provided, however, that the children of any deceased Beneficiary shall collectively have only one vote.

Trustees may be compensated if they choose at the customary rate paid to professional bank trustees for similar services. Trustees may divide their duties among themselves as they may agree in writing. Successor Co-Trustees, absent written agreement, must unanimously agree on Trust decisions.

Family members who are serving as trustees usually do not expect a separate fee to be paid to them. If, however, the named trustee is not also a beneficiary, most people have no objection to paying them for wrapping up the trust or carrying out its terms if it is to continue on for a time. This can be a flat fee that you can specify or may be a percentage of the trust estate, typically around 2 percent. It really would depend upon how complex the trust asset structure is and how long the trust is supposed to continue. Remember that if you name your attorney as the successor trustee, she is going to be charging hourly at attorney rates.

Trustee as a Fiduciary

Under the laws of many states, the trustee of a trust has a legal duty to be a fiduciary in regards to trust transactions. These fiduciary duties include:

1. Duty of loyalty—The trustee must act solely in the interests of the beneficiary in carrying out the stated intent of the grantor of the trust.
2. Duty of prudence—The trustee must make conservative and prudent investment decisions without significant risk to the trust assets.
3. The trustee must be impartial in dealing with multiple beneficiaries.
4. The trustee must not engage in self-dealing or comingle trust assets with her personal assets.
5. The trustee must account to and inform beneficiaries of trust financial transactions including accounting for income, account balances, and expenses.

These duties should be specified in the trust document, although it might be sufficient to specify that the trustee is appointed with the direction and intention that she is under a fiduciary duty to the beneficiaries, since the word "fiduciary" has a settled legal meaning. Some state laws already state that a trustee is a fiduciary.

PERSONAL PROPERTY:
HOW TO DIVIDE UP YOUR STUFF

One of the biggest problems in winding up estates is the "stuff"—all the furniture, garage contents, collections, family photos, and so forth. It is a time-consuming job, and if there are multiple heirs, disagreements and hard feelings can create long-lasting family problems. I have had to litigate personal property divisions because people can get stubborn over items that have seemingly little cash value. A couple of examples:

Dad died. Mom had predeceased him. The two children did not get along at all. The primary problem was the family photos. They were in two cardboard boxes in the possession of the son. He was willing to give his sister some of them, but only the few that he chose. She wanted half and wanted her choice. After lots of fruitless negotiation, I finally brought it in front of a judge. I explained my client's thinking, and the other attorney reiterated that of his client. Being a judge can sometimes be simple. He did the King Solomon solution. His words, which caused the siblings to decide to solve the problem themselves, were as follows:

"Where are these pictures?"

"Right here, your Honor," I said, pointing to them at my feet.

"Okay. Empty them on the table. Make a pile."

I dumped both boxes out on the plaintiff's table. They were loose, not in albums, and some spilled onto the floor.

"Now, I want you to stir them up as best you can, then shove half on one end of the table and half on the other end. You don't have to count them; a guesstimate is fine."

I did that.

"Okay," said the judge, "The pile on the left goes to the sister, the pile on the right to the brother. Next case."

That's why we have judges. This was some time ago—nowadays I think the judge would order them digitized so two copies would be easily available.

Here is a sample of what I put in trusts to cover this situation:

Personal Property Distribution:
The Trustee must follow the directions of the Grantor as to the distribution of personal property attached as a signed or handwritten listing which is incorporated into this Trust Instrument, regarding the disposition of specific items of personal property or groups of personal property (for

example, "All fishing equipment") of every kind including but not limited to furniture, appliances, furnishings, artwork, kitchenware, silverware, glass, books, jewelry, wearing apparel. Any personal property and household effects of the Grantors not listed shall be distributed pro rata in value in the same shares as all other trust assets. The Trustee shall decide on a method of dividing such unlisted assets such as selection by taking turns or by public auction or private sale. The list may be amended from time to time provided it is either notarized or written in the Grantor's handwriting.

TRUSTEE POWERS

The section of a trust spelling out specific powers of a trustee typically runs to several pages as written by most attorneys and as found in form books. However, in carrying out actions on behalf of the trust, banks, brokers, and title insurance companies usually require a notarized form specifying the trustee's authorization to carry out the particular transaction they are dealing with. For example, in selling real estate, the title company will want an affidavit stating that the trustee has the power to sell real estate owned by the trust. The affidavit generally has to be dated close to the date of the proposed sale so that the title company is satisfied that the trust document has not been amended in such a way as to limit that power. Some title companies and banks want to be given an entire copy of the trust, including all amendments.

Two things are problematic about that. The first is privacy. The title company does not need to see to whom you are leaving your assets at your death and any restrictions or limits on the inheritances. That's your business and has nothing to do with the sale of the property. The second is that trusts are often thirty or forty pages long, and the full document will likely have to be recorded as evidence of the trustee's power to make a legitimate and insurable sale.

What I do is include a separate all-inclusive paragraph spelling out a laundry list of specific trustee powers to cover the most likely kinds of transactions in which the trustee might engage. By including this single paragraph in a one- or two-page Affidavit of Trust (also sometimes called a Trust Certificate), you will have provided the necessary information in a concise manner that will not give out unnecessary information and will be inexpensive to record. Title companies often have their own forms for this purpose.

Here is a sample of this general statement of powers (this is not a complete list of all powers contained in the document) that usually satisfies those with whom you are transacting business:

> Any Trustee/Grantor has the power and authority to manage and control, buy, sell, and transfer the Trust property, in such manner as the Trustee may deem advisable, and shall have, enjoy, and exercise all powers and rights over and concerning said property and the proceeds thereof as fully and amply as though said Trustee were the absolute and qualified owner of same, including the power to grant, bargain, sell and convey, encumber and hypothecate real and personal property, and the power to invest in corporate obligations of every kind, stocks, preferred or common, and to buy stocks, bonds, and similar investments on margin or other leveraged accounts, except to the extent that such management would cause includability of an irrevocable trust in the Estate of a Trustee.

EARLY OR PARTIAL DISTRIBUTIONS OF ASSETS TO HEIRS

The short-form description of the duties of a trustee after the death of the grantor is to identify and gather the assets and debts of the grantor and distribute them as instructed in the trust. Sometimes this takes a while and heirs don't want to wait. Also, a trustee has a duty to manage the assets responsibly, which may include investing as appropriate to earn available interest on cash accounts.

The usual cause for delay is being unable to liquidate assets quickly. Often there is real estate that needs to be sold so that the money can be distributed to the heirs. But it might take many months or even years to find a buyer. In the meantime, the other trust assets will be on deposit somewhere earning taxable interest, which leads to accounting fees and taxable income.

Having a paragraph in the trust that allows the trustee to make early distributions to the heirs eliminates some of the beneficiary unrest and allows them to get at least some of their inheritance right away. The trustee needs to hold back a reserve to cover expenses that might be incurred while waiting for a real estate sale, since if she distributes everything except the real estate then it might be difficult to collect the pro-rata shares of future expenses from them, such as property taxes, utilities, insurance, and repairs.

As to specific bequests of personal property, there would be no reason to wait on handing those out. If the grantor designated things like an automobile to a particular person or specific items listed on an attachment to the trust that are to go to a particular person, the trustee would likely be safe in handing out those things.

Here is a sample of what I put in trusts to cover this situation:

Partial Distributions to Trust Beneficiaries:
After the death of Grantor, the Trustee shall have the authority, in his or her absolute discretion, to make partial distributions of Trust assets to the Beneficiaries named in this Trust on a pro-rata basis, prior to the complete distribution of the Trust assets according to its terms. The Trustee shall also have the authority to retain in the name of the Trust a portion of the Trust assets for contemplated expenses during the interim between the death of the Grantor and final distribution.

SPENDTHRIFTS, SALE OF EXPECTED INHERITANCE
We all know people who are not good money managers. To protect them from themselves, we often structure their inheritance so that it is apportioned to them in installments or held in trust

for them under someone else's control. There are companies actively soliciting those who are willing to sell their share of trust funds, usually at a huge discount. Allowing a beneficiary to sell their expected inheritance defeats the whole purpose of the grantor in leaving them the money in this manner. So, we make it impossible for them to thwart the grantor's intention by including a provision such as this:

Spendthrift Provision:
Neither the principal nor the income of the Trust shall be liable for the debts of a Beneficiary. Except as otherwise expressly provided in this Agreement, no Beneficiary of any Trust shall have any right, power, or authority to alienate, encumber, assign, sell, gift, or hypothecate his or her interest in the principal or income of this Trust in any manner, nor shall the interests of any Beneficiary be subject to the claims of his or her creditors or liable to attachment, execution, or other process of law. The limitations herein shall not restrict the exercise of any right to disclaim an inheritance.

ARBITRATION OF DISPUTES

Sometimes there are those who are not pleased with the decisions made by the grantor of a trust. Especially if they were left less from the distribution than they expected, or received nothing at all. Finding a lawyer and suing is the most likely thing they are going to do, and this can cause additional expense to the trust as well as taking more time to settle things. I like an arbitration clause in a case like that since it is typically less expensive and quicker than going through court proceedings and you can require that the person challenging the trust pay for all costs of arbitration, including the expenses of the trustee and her lawyer if they are unsuccessful. I also like to see a disinheritance clause that states that anyone challenging the trust successfully is entitled to nothing at all from the trust. The disinheritance clause is probably not always going to be successful since a court can overrule any trust provisions, but just the fact that it is written into the trust might discourage people from attempting a challenge.

Resolution of Conflict:

Any controversy between the Trustee and any other Trustee or Trustees, or between any other parties to this Trust, including Beneficiaries, involving the construction or application of any of the terms, provisions, or conditions of this Trust shall, on the written request of either or any disagreeing party served on the other or others, be submitted to arbitration. The parties to such arbitration shall each appoint one person to hear and determine the dispute and, if they are unable to agree, then the two persons so chosen shall select a third impartial arbitrator whose decision shall be final and conclusive upon both parties. The cost of arbitration shall be borne by the losing party. Such arbitration shall comply with the commercial arbitration rules of the American Arbitration Association, New York Regional Office, 150 East 42nd St, Floor 17, New York, NY 10017.

Incontestability:

The beneficial provisions of this Trust Agreement are intended to be in lieu of any other rights, claims, or interests of whatsoever nature, whether statutory or otherwise, except bona fide pre-death debts, which any Beneficiary hereunder may have in Grantor's Estate or in the properties in trust hereunder. Accordingly, if any Beneficiary hereunder asserts any claim (except a legally enforceable debt), statutory election, or other right or interest against or in Grantor's Estate, or any properties of this Trust, other than pursuant to the express terms hereof, or directly or indirectly contests, disputes, or calls into question, before any court, the validity of this Trust Agreement, then:

    a. Such Beneficiary shall thereby absolutely forfeit any and all beneficial interests of whatsoever kind and nature which such Beneficiary or his or her heirs might otherwise have under this Trust Agreement and the interests of the other Beneficiaries hereunder shall thereupon be appropriately and proportionately increased; and

b. All of the provisions of this Trust Agreement, to the extent that they confer any benefits, powers, or rights whatsoever upon such claiming, electing, or contesting Beneficiary, shall thereupon become absolutely void; and

c. Such claiming, electing, or contesting Beneficiary, if then acting as a Trustee hereunder, shall automatically cease to be a Trustee and shall thereafter be ineligible either to select, remove, or become a Trustee hereunder.

THE TRUST FUNDING SUMMARY/LIST OF ASSETS

One problem we have after a person dies is locating his or her assets. There is always a fear that we didn't find all the things that the deceased owned. Part of your trust should be a simple form added as an addendum for informational purposes where you list all the things transferred into the trust name and when you made the transfers. The list can be updated by hand as you divest assets or add new ones to the trust. This would include beneficiary designations for insurance policies and accounts, title transfers, TOD and POD designations, deeds and leases, business interests, and investment accounts. Some accounts, for example, are only found online because you have opted for no mailed statements, so it's a good idea to list the online brokerage and other accounts along with passwords so that they can be accessed.

DISINHERITING FAMILY MEMBERS

If a person makes a will and doesn't leave something to his or her child, the legal assumption is that it must be a mistake, since people will normally include the so-called objects of their affection. The omitted child can challenge the will and take a share. Now, if the will specifically says they are intentionally omitting the child, most states will follow the intent of the maker of the will and leave the child out. These rules do not apply in a trust, since we state specifically that only the people named in the trust are heirs, and if someone happens to be omitted, then it was done intentionally.

Section 7.03. Specific Omissions:
Any and all persons and entities, except those persons and entities specifically named herein, have been intentionally omitted from this Trust Agreement. If any person or entity shall successfully challenge any term or condition of this Trust Agreement, then to that person or entity shall be given the sum of one dollar ($1.00) in lieu and in place of any other benefit, grant, or interest which that person or interest may have in the Trust Estate.

This provision can also apply to a spouse unless state law provides a guaranteed share of trust assets to an omitted spouse. In a will, the testator cannot disinherit his or her spouse. The surviving spouse is typically given a so-called *right of election* or *forced share*, which means he can take what was given to him under the will or take a share specified by statute, which is generally what he would have inherited had there been no will at all. In most states that do not have community property laws, the forced share rule does not apply to trusts, so you can disinherit your spouse from all trust assets. Check with your lawyer if this is your intent to see if local law allows it. There are a surprising number of married couples who have separate assets and separate trusts and estate plans, so this is not necessarily unusual or underhanded.

CREDITORS AND DEBTS

In a probated estate, the personal representative in charge of the estate is required to not only notify known creditors of the deceased of the ongoing probate, but also must publish notice to unknown possible creditors. This gives creditors a time limit for filing a claim to be paid for what is legally owed them. The personal representative can approve the claims or deny them, in which case the creditor can ask the court to rule on the claim's validity. Heirs and executors like this procedure since it eliminates the chance of a claim being made against the estate months or years after the case is closed and the funds distributed. It creates a short statute of limitations. Anyone who has been hospitalized knows that medical bills sometimes show up months after the medical procedures have been performed. With the death of the local newspaper in so many communities, the publication rule is out of step with reality, but there are legal newspapers that can still accept classified advertisements.

It is a good idea to run a credit check on the deceased, which might reveal creditors that no one knew existed. Of course, all credit cards should be immediately canceled and all subscriptions and recurring payments stopped.

Some states have expanded this protection to trusts, and with that in mind I always put the publication requirement in the trust language. If, however, we know that the law has not been extended to trusts in our state and there is a chance that late claims might be made, we can open a probate for some of the assets that are not passing through the trust to take advantage of the publication protection on claims. The bulk of the assets would then pass as usual through the trust.

Trustee's Notice to Creditors:
If no personal representative of Grantor's Estate has been appointed so that the publication and notice requirements with respect to creditors have not been discharged, Trustee shall, to the extent required by law, publish and serve notice to all creditors in the same manner as required for a personal representative. Trustee shall pay, to the extent required by law, all proper claims allowed by the Trustee or a court having jurisdiction.

The notice procedure and its protections are one of the advantages of probate promoted by probate attorneys.

In many states trusts now have the same ability to publish notice to creditors, known and unknown, and receive the same protection as probated estates, so that advantage no longer exists.

Debts payable by the probated estate can include unexpected claims, such as might be made by the state. *Estate Recovery* refers to a state law that allows the state to claim repayment of government benefits, such as Medicaid for nursing home care, from a deceased person's probated estate. While not all states allow this, where it exists, repayment can completely deplete the probate estate accounts, leaving nothing for the heirs. This can be avoided by having no probate case filed, since the law refers to claims against the estate and not against non-probated assets such as those assets in the name of a trust. This is another reason to avoid probate.

THE TRUST PROTECTOR

Best trust idea ever.

As I have said, creating a trust has become the number-one favored method of avoiding probate and ensuring that the assets are left to beneficiaries in the simplest, safest, and least expensive possible manner. One possible problem with trusts in the past has been making sure that the named trustee carries out the management and distribution of the trust in accordance with the grantor's wishes and directions. Without court supervision, trustees might not handle the job efficiently, quickly, or even honestly. Self-dealing can be an issue benefiting the trustee but harming the interests of the beneficiaries. Once the trust principal is spent, stolen, or wasted, the money is difficult or impossible to recover. A trust protector is a person or firm whom you name in the trust document to oversee the actions of the trustee in carrying out your directions.

If the trust assets consist largely of real estate, for example, the trustee could have his own relatives or himself, if he is a real estate agent, list the properties for sale and collect commissions of the sale of the property without necessarily getting the best price possible. That would be a conflict of interest that the trust protector could veto. The trustee should not be profiting from trust transactions. The same is true of investment decisions with the trust assets. Being a fiduciary means no speculative investments. Having someone watch over the trustee's actions, and requiring the trustee to account to another person for what has been done or is going to be done, gives the trust beneficiaries a layer of protection against trustee malfeasance or misfeasance.

Traditionally a trust protector has been used in irrevocable trusts to provide for the long-term carrying out of the objectives of the original trust grantor. A trust set up for children, which then continues on for the grandchildren and even further for great-grandchildren, is a typical type of irrevocable trust benefiting successive generations. The purpose might be to provide income to trust beneficiaries, educational expenses, operation of family businesses, or even managing recreational real estate for their benefit. The grantor needs to be clear as to the irrevocable trust's intended purpose.

Nowadays we sometimes recommend the use of a trust protector even in revocable trusts that are to become irrevocable at the death of the grantor, as most do, and then are to be immediately distributed. Having co-trustees can lessen the need for a trust protector, presumably because they watch each other.

Who can or should the trust protector be? First, it should not be a trust beneficiary or the attorney for the trustee or for the grantor. The attorney for the grantor is sometimes appointed but this is a grave mistake, since there is a potential conflict of interest if the attorney is the one who drafted the trust. The best choice, in my opinion, is either a professional trust company or the trust division of a bank. They would have to agree to the appointment and will want a copy of the trust document. I have no opinion on professional trust protection companies since they are new and don't have a track record to examine.

The powers of a trust protector should be set out in detail in the trust document. Here are some common powers that should be included. Just because they have been given these powers does not mean they will have to exercise all of them.

1. The power to remove or replace trustees. Trustees are usually family members and may not carry out the duties of trustee in an efficient or honest manner. Some are just lazy. With a trust protector there is someone to advise the trustee and prod them to get things done in accordance with the grantor's intention and the trust instructions. If they are not doing the job, then the trust protector should have the power to remove or replace them.

2. Settling disputes between co-trustees and/or beneficiaries. The trust protector can act as a referee and final word if there are disputes regarding distribution of assets, sale prices, investments, or timing of distributions.

3. In long-term trusts, the trust protector should have the power to change the terms of the trust if there is a change in the law or taxation significant enough to impact the trust purposes.

4. The trust should specify that both the trustees and the trust protectors are to act in a fiduciary capacity toward the trust beneficiary. Some state laws do say that, while others presume that the roles are fiduciary. Having the trust state that fiduciary status gives the beneficiaries protection and legal recourse if the trustees and trust protectors do not act in a fiduciary manner.

5. The trustee should be required to have the trust protector approve all investment and distribution decisions.

6. Trust protectors should be compensated, and the manner and amount of compensation should be stated. Referring to the fees charged by schedule of a professional bank trustee or protector gives some guidelines.

There are lots of other specific powers that are often included by the drafter of a trust. The nature of the trust assets as well as the trust grantor's intentions will determine how detailed these powers need to be. If the trust is a special-needs type, which extends for the lifetime of a special-needs beneficiary, particular care should be taken to protect the assets for the beneficiary without affecting other benefits to which he might be entitled. Similarly, a trust set up to manage family-owned businesses will have its own set of specific powers different from those that are managing only investment assets.

My advice to have your final trust document reviewed by another attorney is reiterated here. A second opinion, preferably set out in an opinion letter, is a very good idea.

CHAPTER FOUR

Six Situations When a Trust Is Absolutely Necessary

Probate avoidance is a good reason to create a trust, but suppose avoiding probate is not a concern to you? Even if you are able to avoid probate using one of the methods described in chapter 2 of this book, a trust may be necessary for other reasons due to your family circumstances.

1. **Minor Children.** If you have no trust but have minor children, at the death of the parents any sizeable inheritance going to the children will be managed by a court-appointed conservator and the balance turned over to the child upon attaining the age of majority, usually age eighteen. This is not a result most parents hope for. A trust, on the other hand, would allow you to put a person of your choice in charge of the money without courts, and would allow you to specify at what age and under what conditions the money would ultimately be given to the child.

2. **Disabled Beneficiaries.** The type of disability is the concern here. If it is just a manageable physical disability with no public assistance involved and the person is of age, then no special trust provisions would need to be made. However, mental impairment could require that someone other than the heir manage their money for them. If they are also receiving need-based governmental

assistance such as Medicaid, leaving the money directly and immediately to them could disqualify them for their benefits and require that they use up the inherited money for their medical care and then reapply for those same benefits when the money is depleted. It won't take long. As explained earlier, a special-needs trust will allow the money to be used for the beneficiary's benefit without affecting his or her existing benefits. Any money left over after the beneficiary's death can be directed to another named beneficiary.

3. **Spendthrifts.** Even non-disabled adults may need someone to manage their money for them. I have had a few clients whose attitudes were that if an heir blows their share of the money left to them, then that is their problem and they are not going to try and control people's lives from beyond the grave. Okay, that's a choice. But most clients opt to set up a plan for those likely to need it. Perhaps their share continues to be held in trust for their lifetime but can be used at the discretion of the trustee for ordinary living expenses with some sort of regular allowance provided. It's your money and you can set up any plan you like. Heirs are not required to accept the gift in trust and can disclaim it if they choose. People sometimes set up stringent and even unusual requirements for beneficiaries. They may require graduation from college or trade school or passing intermittent drug tests, or going on church-sponsored missions. It's all up to you.

4. **Unmarried Couples.** The law does not provide the same rights and privileges to unmarried couples as it gives to those who are married. And surviving families are often not sympathetic to the surviving non-spouse. If you want your partner to be able to continue to live in your house and use the furniture, vehicles, and maybe the vacation condo and bank accounts, you have to provide a legal apparatus to be sure that happens. Putting

everything in trust with specific instructions as to what rights the surviving partner may have in the assets in your name is critical. And be sure the partner is named on a medical power of attorney, since some medical care facilities will only allow ICU visitation or medical decision-making by family members if not otherwise specified.

5. **Blended Families.** It is very common nowadays that people with children remarry someone who has their own children, and the couple might even then have more children together. Without proper trust planning, it becomes a gamble as to who gets what share of the family assets at the death of one partner or both.

Let's say you have two adult children and your spouse has three. Then the two of you have another child. Unfortunately, you die before the youngest reaches adulthood. Let's assume all assets are jointly owned and that you and your spouse are each other's beneficiary. At your death everything goes to your partner, and at your partner's death everything goes to his or her children with the share of the minor child being held in a court-ordered conservatorship. Your adult children receive nothing. If your spouse dies before you, the same result, except her adult children receive nothing.

When I explain this to people, they invariably say that they would never cut off the children of their spouse. Who would do that? The fact is that at the death of one the survivor is likely to remarry, probably with someone with his or her own children, and the former stepchildren are soon forgotten. Happens all the time. Making a trust can eliminate this unwanted result. It is helpful to have answers to all the what-if scenarios.

6. **Separated Couples and/or Separate Assets.** Often, particularly in second marriages, each partner will have his or her own set of assets that are not jointly owned. They may not agree on how these assets are to

be distributed at their deaths and so a joint trust will not work for them. Especially if a couple are separated but not divorced, they may prefer to do their own estate planning separate from their spouse. This is perfectly appropriate and they often do make some provision for their partner, with the balance going to heirs of their choice. A trust is the best way to do this, since with a will, or no will at all, probate court laws give a surviving spouse statutory rights to elect against a will, homestead allowances, spousal shares, and exempt property rights. Community property laws in a few states further complicate their estate planning situation. With a trust or two trusts, they can coordinate their estate plans and, depending on state law, all or most of those rights do not apply, keeping their intentions intact.

CHAPTER FIVE

Using Powers of Attorney to Avoid Court-Ordered Guardians and Conservators

All states have laws that provide for protection and care of adults and minors who cannot, due to age or mental and/or physical impairment, care for themselves. The two types of court-ordered care are guardianship, where someone is appointed to take care of the day-to-day and physical needs of a person; and conservatorship, where someone is appointed to manage the money of a minor or disabled adult. These are good laws and necessary in a society that takes care of those who cannot care for themselves. However, this care comes with significant side effects.

Court oversight is the perceived advantage of both guardianships and conservatorships. Judges take a very conservative view of the dealings of conservators. They are held to stringent rules in many cases as to what expenditures and investments are approved as appropriate. Some courts will only allow the funds being managed to be put into low or no-interest bank accounts at specific banks. The conservator might believe that a particular expenditure is reasonable based on the amount of money being held, but the court might disagree. As an example, I saw a case where the conservator for a seventeen-year-old wanted to buy a car for the teenager to go to and from school. There was a fund approaching three-quarters of a million dollars from an aunt's estate being held for her. The conservator, who was the teenager's mother, just wanted to buy a used car. The judge vetoed the idea as not necessary.

Had the girl's money been held in trust for her with the girl's mother as trustee, rather than conservator, there would have been no court oversight and no judge's agreement would have been needed. This was a failure of estate planning on the aunt's behalf.

Conservatorships for adults who are incapacitated are similarly unneeded if the incapacitated person has set up a durable power of attorney and a trust. Since the person named as POA and trustee could legally transact business and manage the money of the disabled person on a fiduciary basis, no court-ordered conservatorship would be needed.

This is important because in many states anyone can petition the local adult protective services branch of government to file for a conservatorship if there is evidence that the person needs protection. Typically, these petitions are filed to stop someone from mismanaging or taking the adult's assets.

The petition for conservatorship or guardianship can be contested by the person who would be the subject of the guardian/conservator petition (the ward), and evidence of the existence of a power of attorney and trust could defeat the petition. Upon filing the petition, the court appoints a *guardian ad litem* (guardian at law or GAL), usually an attorney, who then visits the alleged incapacitated person (the ward of the court, if the petition is successful) and files a written report with the court detailing the ward's condition. This GAL is supposed to protect the rights of the allegedly incapacitated person. All at attorney fee rates, of course.

It might be that the GAL reports to the court and says no permanent guardian or conservator is needed, but this too can be contested and witnesses, including the ward, can be brought in to testify. The problem is that even if the petition is defeated, and no permanent guardian is appointed, the subject of the petition has to pay the fees of the court-appointed GAL. Even though they win, they lose. It's better to cut this off early by disclosing the documents to the court that eliminate the need for a conservator and guardian. Judges are typically happy to not increase their own caseload and may summarily dismiss the petition. I have used this tactic successfully.

USING POWERS OF ATTORNEY TO DEFEAT PROBATE COURT CONSERVATORSHIPS

A power of attorney is basically just a permission slip giving someone the legal authority to do things for you. It might be limited to a particular transaction such as buying or selling a piece of real estate, with the power ending when the transaction is completed. Or it might be to do any kind of business on your behalf unlimited in time or scope and ends when either it is rescinded or you die. It could be to make medical decisions for you, including end-of-life decisions.

A so-called springing power of attorney is one that only becomes effective upon the occurrence of a particular action or situation. Mental or physical incapacity is the most common type of occurrence that allows a power of attorney to spring into effect. This avoids the need to go to court to transact business on behalf of someone temporarily or permanently mentally disabled. How to determine incapacity is spelled out in the POA document. Note that the trust document contains similar language and gives a successor trustee similar powers over trust assets. Be sure that these two do not conflict. It is far better practice to have one person fulfill both roles. Here is one example:

Until I am certified as incapacitated as provided hereunder, this Power of Attorney shall have no force or effect. All authority granted in this Power of Attorney shall be subject to establishment of incapacity as provided hereunder. For purposes of establishing incapacity, whenever two licensed, practicing medical doctors who are not related to me or to any beneficiary or heir at law by blood or marriage certify in writing that I am unable to manage my financial affairs because of mental or physical infirmity and the certificates are personally served upon me, then the attorney(s)-in-fact named herein shall assume all powers granted in this Power of Attorney.

Anyone dealing with the attorney(s)-in-fact may rely upon written medical certificates or a photocopy of them presented to them along with the original Power of Attorney document, and shall incur no liability for any dealings with any designated attorney(s)-in-fact in good faith reliance on said certificate and the original Power of Attorney document. This provision is inserted in this document to encourage third parties to deal with my attorney(s)-in-fact without the need for court proceedings.

This is not language carved in stone. You might specify one doctor rather than two, or a particular type of physician specialty. Lawyers will likely write the provision differently, but the intent and legal effect is the same. The person named as attorney-in-fact has no authority to do anything unless and until the criteria for determining incapacity are met.

This type of POA is also called a durable power of attorney, since it stays effective even after a person is deemed incompetent. In that case the following sentence is used, which refers to the durable nature of the document:

After this Power of Attorney becomes effective, it shall not be affected by any subsequent incapacity which I may hereafter suffer or the passage of time.

The reason we use the durable language is because a POA by definition gives the agent the power to do anything that the person giving the power could legally do. If a person becomes incapacitated, they are no longer legally able to enter into contracts or sign legal documents, so the agent who is acting as the principal's surrogate would likewise have no power to do those things.

Not all POAs have the springing language. If it is left out, the power is effective when the document is signed and delivered to the attorney-in-fact. There are good reasons why you might not want the springing power. A person who is elderly or medically disabled, still mentally competent, but who needs help conducting their normal business dealings such as taxes, paying bills, or managing investments will often use an immediate POA.

A probate court-supervised conservatorship is not necessary when a person has a properly prepared POA. The purpose of a conservatorship is to protect and manage the assets of those who are incapacitated and/or mentally incompetent and cannot take care of their own financial affairs. Combined with a revocable trust and a medical power of attorney, the court will likely not appoint either a guardian or a conservator.

MEDICAL POWERS OF ATTORNEY AS A WAY OF AVOIDING ADULT GUARDIANSHIPS

Just as disabled or incompetent people might need someone to handle their business affairs, they usually need someone to do medical decision-making for them, such as consenting to hospitalization or surgery. All medical and dental decisions need to be made as well as decisions regarding end-of-life situations. Should life support be terminated or continued? What religious objections might a person have to certain procedures or drugs, and who is going to make these known? Even things that need to be done like picking up prescriptions or dealing with health insurance, Medicare, or Medicaid.

If the person has no medical power of attorney or advance directive, physicians and hospitals might well refuse to listen to family members regarding serious health issues. Liability is a big deal to health-care workers, and they may insist on a court-ordered guardianship to protect themselves. Once a person becomes incapacitated, it is too late to sign the documents naming a health-care advocate. The only recourse then is to the courts if the medical facility will not accept the family's making medical decisions without the written medical directive.

Most states and many hospitals have fill-in-the-blank forms for a medical power of attorney. In some states a physician can appoint a health-care surrogate to make medical decisions for a disabled patient who has no health-care POA, but it is always better to be able to have a person you choose to make those decisions.

CHAPTER SIX

Selecting and Dealing with Attorneys

After reading this book and possibly *Living Trusts for Everyone*, you will be familiar with basic estate planning strategies, including the difference between trusts and wills and the basics of probate avoidance. As I stated earlier, I do not recommend writing your own trust or downloading one and filling in the blanks. My advice is to fill out the information form in Appendix D and take it with you for an attorney consultation. Finding a specialist in trusts can be fairly easy in states where the bar association certifies that specialty. In other states, you are kind of on your own since all you would have to go on is the lawyer's word that they know what they are doing.

Try interviewing more than one lawyer to see how they would recommend setting up your estate plan, how long it will take, and what will be the approximate cost. Do not agree to an open-ended hourly rate since you will often find the cost to be greater than the estimate. It's unlikely to be less. Sign an attorney fee agreement once you have settled on the lawyer selection. Many states require these of lawyers. Sometimes the initial interview is free, but not always. There are many attorneys who will give you a flat rate after talking to you for a complete package, which, if it is a revocable trust-based plan, should include the following:

1. The trust document itself. This includes all of your decisions regarding the trust, including who will be the

trustees after your death, the shares to be distributed to each beneficiary, and standard legal provisions to make the trust work, as well as detailed descriptions of any restrictions on when and how distributions will be made to the beneficiaries.

2. The personal property distribution list in which you can designate particular items to go to particular people.

3. A durable power of attorney for each grantor, either an immediate durable power of attorney or a springing power of attorney effective on your disability as defined in the document.

4. A medical power of attorney and advance directives. This can include a so-called living will to set out your wishes as to providing life support in terminal situations. The people named as your medical decision-makers can be different than your successor trustees.

5. Pour-over will to direct any assets that are not yet in the trust name to the trust as well as appointing a guardian for minor children.

6. Instructions for funding the trust as well as sample forms for making the transfers.

7. Deeds from you to your trust for all real estate. If there is property you own outside your state of residence, your attorney will have to either be licensed in that jurisdiction or have an attorney or title company in that state prepare the deed. Otherwise probate will be necessary for each state in which you own real estate.

After the attorney interviews you, will have a pretty good idea if they know what they are talking about. You should feel comfortable with them. If the lawyer will agree, see if you can get a draft copy of all documents to review before signing anything other than the attorney fee agreement. These documents are of necessity detailed so as to cover foreseeable situations, and you can't be expected to read all of them while sitting in the lawyer's conference room.

CHAPTER SEVEN

Funding the Trust

INITIAL FUNDING

Once your trust is signed, your attorney will have you sign a few documents to start the funding process.

A pour-over will (see Appendix F) is signed for each grantor and has two purposes. First, it is a backup document that transfers all assets that are in your names at your deaths to the trust. However, as mentioned earlier, we do not want to use the will for that purpose, since our plan is to have all assets already in the name of the trust at your deaths. Probate avoidance is one of the purposes of the trust and we do not want to probate the will. Second, if you have minor children at the time of your deaths, or a disabled child who is under a court-appointed guardianship, the will is used to appoint the people of your choice to be their guardians.

As discussed earlier, my strong recommendation is to not use the pour-over will as a means of funding the trust. If your attorney recommends this, I would get another attorney's advice before signing anything.

Deeds will have been prepared transferring all your interests in real estate to the trust name. Out-of-state property should be taken care of at this time by signing the deeds prepared by the other state's lawyer. The deed will be from you and your spouse, or co-owner if not married, to the trust. It could read, for example:

Grantor, John H. Doe, an unmarried man, quit-claims to the John H. Doe Revocable Trust u/a dated April 1, 2021.

The legal (land) description and all other required parts of the deed will of course have to be included, and it will be notarized and often witnessed. A married couple must both sign the deed even if the property is in only one name.

Personal property is assigned to the trust with an assignment form (Appendix G). This is just a document stating your intention that any personal property—including but not limited to furniture, household goods, machinery, tools, lawn equipment, farm implements, jewelry, artworks, collections, animals, and intangibles such as contract rights, patents, trademarks, royalty rights, manuscripts, and any other non-titled asset owned now or acquired in the future—is intended to be trust property. It should be notarized and kept with all your other trust documents.

Investment accounts, deposit and bank accounts, CDs, money market accounts, insurance policies, bonds, stocks, or brokerage accounts will be assigned into the trust name, or the trust can be named the beneficiary of the account if you wish. The companies managing these will have their own forms in most cases, written with the language and provisions they prefer. You can request the forms ahead of time so that they can be signed contemporaneously with the other paperwork. It is sometimes necessary to go to the bank or office to complete these transfers. Make sure that they understand that this is not to be considered a sale and repurchase of the asset, merely a name change. No capital gains tax should be incurred, and the tax basis should not be changed. Your broker is not entitled to a transaction fee for making this change.

Vehicles and watercraft, as well as recreational vehicles and mobile homes, will have titles and can be retitled in the trust name at your local tax office or secretary of state office—whichever agency handles that sort of thing. It will likely take a personal visit to do this.

In earlier chapters I described ways to leave assets to particular people by way of joint ownership and beneficiary designation. You can do that with some assets and have the trust own everything else. You may, for example, put an automobile in joint ownership with right of survivorship to someone instead of putting it in the trust name. It would then go automatically on your death to that person while the trust assets are distributed to another set of heirs. Or, suppose you want everything divided equally among your children except for a particular account or insurance policy, which you want to go to a grandchild. A beneficiary designation could take care of that without the grandchild having to wait for the trust to be distributed.

Union, employee, or association benefits. Oftentimes unions, banks, credit cards, and associations will provide death benefits to members such as term life insurance. However, if these are not claimed, then they lapse. Be sure to assign these to your trust, or at the very least make your chosen trustee aware that they exist. The same is true of stock options and even unused vacation time from your employer. These are all assets that should be part of your estate.

AN ONGOING PROCESS

After the last meeting with your attorney, you should have the original signed trust document in your possession. You will have transferred all your assets into the trust name in one of the methods explained in this book. But that is not the end of it. Things change; people move, get new jobs, open new bank accounts, get new investments. Life is not static. So it is very important that you review your trust periodically to be sure the trust is still fully funded. Otherwise the non-funded assets would have to be probated, and you will have defeated one of the purposes for which you created the trust.

Do not sign a power of attorney allowing your lawyer to sign your name to asset transfer documents. Doing so gives the attorney complete access and control of all you own. While doing so might be presented as a way of saving you time and trouble, it is not worth the risk that something might happen in the lawyer's interest and not your own. If you want to go ahead anyway, have an attorney not associated with your lawyer's office draft the power of attorney so that it is limited in time or scope. Your lawyer has a conflict of interest in preparing the power of attorney as well as being the attorney-in-fact. Plus, you would be paying him legal fees to do clerical work that you can do yourself for free.

THE ANNUAL REVIEW

Some attorneys schedule annual appointments, just as dentists do, to review your trust and update it if necessary. Of course, they charge for these services even if nothing has changed and nothing new needs to be done. Unless something significant has happened in your family relationships or your intentions as expressed in the trust, the only time you might need to see a lawyer is if funding documents need to be prepared; a deed for newly acquired property, for example. Most of the time you can fill out things like beneficiary designations and title transfers without legal help. Years ago, I actually met with groups of banks and estate planners to explain trusts and trust funding requests that they might run into, since trusts were not widely used at that time. Nowadays you will not be met with blank stares when you request that an asset be funded into your trust in one way or another. The business community is now pretty well versed in trusts and will often be able to suggest the best way to proceed.

Your annual review should be conducted on a date that's easy to remember. At that time, you can pull out your list of assets funded into the trust and verify that there is nothing new to add. A new deed might need to be prepared or POD and TOD forms filled out for new accounts.

You should also consider whether changes need to be made to the trust itself. Are the named trustees still appropriate? Are you happy with the distribution provisions and any restrictions on inheritance you previously set up? This is the time to update.

When you had minor children you likely named an adult as the trustee of the trust, but years later you may want to name the children themselves as the trustees to maintain simplicity, reduce costs, and preserve privacy.

Other documents in your estate planning packet might also need to be changed. Sometimes the people named as power of attorney or medical decision-makers move away, die, or are otherwise no longer appropriate for the role you have assigned them. A medical patient advocate, for example, should, if possible, live nearby to be able to talk with physicians and social workers to monitor your health care in critical situations. Perhaps you have changed your mind about organ donation or do-not-resuscitate documents. These documents, while not specifically probate-avoiding, are very pertinent to your personal estate planning and can affect adult guardianship issues.

AVOIDING YOUR PARENTS' PROBATE

Do you expect to inherit? You will be paying for the probate of your parents or others who might leave you something if they don't properly plan. How to approach this? It can be difficult to broach the subject of wills and trusts with parents. Many are reluctant to talk about it and secretive with their financial situation. When questioned they may say something like, "We already have a will, so everything's taken care of."

This is when you can reply easily without seeming to pry by saying, "That's what I thought too, but I went to a lawyer and found out that wills have to be probated, which I didn't know. She set me up with a trust and medical directives so we won't have to go to court when the time comes."

Then give them this book. It is a way of opening the conversation by talking about what you did and why. You won't be sorry.

TRUST SAFEKEEPING

Okay, so everything's signed, everything is transferred to the trust. Now what do you do with all the paperwork?

You are responsible for keeping your documents together and making them findable at your death. When I do trusts, I put everything in a three-ring binder with pockets to store transfer documents and copies of deeds. Still, once in a while I get a call from heirs who cannot find the trust. When I tell them to look for the binder, sometimes they locate it, sometimes not. The attorney does not usually keep the client's documents. We might have a copy, but the originals are taken home with them. The heirs start looking and sometimes are expecting a stack of papers or file folders and not a binder.

Tell your named trustee where you put the trust. Buy a small safe at a discount store to keep it protected from flood or fire. Just tell someone. If the original trust cannot be found, the procedure for re-creating it is troublesome and time-consuming as well as very frustrating for the family. You cannot revoke it by destroying it. If you want to revoke, it please read the section in chapter 3 that tells you how to do it properly.

CHAPTER EIGHT

Myths and Misconceptions about Estates and Probate

1. **A power of attorney can be used to take care of a person's affairs at their death.**

   False. A power of attorney is a document that you sign that gives another person the right to act for you in some or all transactions. If you are dead you do not have the power to do anything, so that means neither does the person to whom you gave the power. The power of attorney dies with you.

2. **Reading of the will. A will has to be read to heirs like on television.**

   False. While all heirs at law and those who are mentioned in the will have to be given a copy of it, there is no requirement of a formal reading where everyone gathers in a room and listens to the lawyer read it aloud. A mailed copy is the usual procedure. As to trusts, unless local law specifies otherwise only those mentioned in the trust need be notified, and even then they are only entitled to see the parts of the trust specific to them.

3. **You can disinherit your spouse and/or children or leave them a pittance.**

   Partly true. Children can be disinherited provided that you clearly say, in writing, that you are intentionally leaving them nothing. Otherwise there is a legal presumption that your children, as your natural objects of affection, would not have been disinherited unless you mistakenly left them out. This is important since there are cases of, for example, a father's children born out of wedlock or from previous marriages. As to a spouse, if you are in a community property state, you cannot disinherit him or her without their written consent. In other states you can't do it through a will, but can sometimes put all assets in your individual trust and leave nothing to the spouse. Check with a good estate planning attorney to see the rules where you live.

4. **Court costs are what makes probate expensive.**
    True and false. Court costs—that is, money paid directly to the court—can be sizeable but are not usually the biggest expense. Courts charge filing fees, guardian ad litem fees, inventory fees on the value of the probated estate, bond fees, and sometimes state inheritance tax. The biggest cost by far is the attorney fee. A more detailed description of attorney fees is referenced in other parts of this book. Suffice it to say here that attorney and executor fees can be many thousands of dollars—money that is paid by the heirs, money they wouldn't have had to pay if they had avoided probate.

5. **If you have a will you don't need to go through probate.** **False but sometimes true.** Wills are just written instructions to the probate court as to who gets what when you die and who is in charge of making that happen. If there are very limited assets, then a probate small estate procedure can be used, avoiding full probate. However, unless your estate qualifies for these procedures, a probate court must oversee the administration of the will in order to legally pass the estate assets to your heirs. This can be very expensive as well as time-consuming. In most cases, your heirs will not receive their share until the probate process is over and all debts and expenses are paid. A will does not usually avoid probate.

6. **The state gets everything if you die without a will.**

   False. The state gets a share if you go through probate whether you have a will or not, but the only time the state gets everything is if the person dying has no known or locatable heirs, or in the event of abandoned property whose ownership cannot be ascertained, in which case it would escheat to the state.

7. **The oldest child gets first shot at being executor.**

   False, unless the oldest child happens to be the one named in a will. In a will situation, the named executor (a.k.a. personal representative) is the one with preference. That person can decline, in which case a second named choice, if any, is the one. If no named person is willing to act as such, then the court will name a public administrator to handle the probate (at attorney fee rates, of course). If there is no will, then the heirs can agree on who will be the executor; lacking agreement, the court will do it. In a trust there is a named trustee as well as a second choice. If properly written, a trust will have a method for choosing a new trustee if the named one refuse to act, dies, or is incompetent. There is no preference given to the eldest child unless you are talking about ascension to the throne.

8. **A handwritten will is not legal.**

   False. All states recognize a handwritten will, which in most cases does not have to comply with statutory signing and witnessing requirements. This is called a holographic will and should be entirely in the handwriting of the deceased except in limited cases. It is also going to be probated if there are probatable assets.

9. **If you have a trust then there is no need for probate.**

   Usually true but not always. Sometimes we want to have a small probate to take advantage of a short statute of limitations on a notice to creditors for creditor claims. So, we might leave some things out of the trust intentionally to take advantage of this statute. However, in many states trusts can now advertise for creditors to appear and also get this short statute of limitations.

10. **Wills can be changed by crossing things off and writing things in by hand so long as you initial the changes in the margin**.

    False. I know people do this and think it is legal, but it is not. You should not take out your will or trust, cross something out or write something in, and initial the change. Doing this could invalidate the document altogether, or at best the handwritten and redacted areas will be ignored. There are specific signing formalities that are required under the laws for legal documents and amendments to those documents, which could include notarizations and a specific number of witnesses.

11. **When my parents die, I have the right to inherit even if they had remarried**.

    False. Except for the rules of intestacy (described in chapter 1), if your parent has remarried and owned everything jointly with the new spouse, at her death you are not entitled to inherit anything—unless of course your parent and the new spouse provided for you specifically in a trust or beneficiary arrangement. Even at the death of your parent's new spouse, you still inherit nothing except as provided by them.

12. **My brother borrowed money from my mom who is now dead. Doesn't he have to pay it back to the estate?**

    It depends. Often the borrower claims the money was a gift and that they still get an equal share of the estate. Unless Mom covered this situation in her estate planning, a question of her intent may have to be decided in court. At the very least, it is likely to create a family rift. We usually suggest language in a trust that says the money should be considered an advance on the borrower's expected inheritance to be deducted from his share.

APPENDIX A

Sample Intestacy Laws

The following is the State of Michigan law on who inherits from a person who dies without a will. Other states have similar statutes.

MICHIGAN INTESTACY LAWS

Intestate estate

1. Any part of a decedent's estate not effectively disposed of by will passes by intestate succession to the decedent's heirs as prescribed in this act, except as modified by the decedent's will.
2. A decedent by will may expressly exclude or limit the right of an individual or class to succeed to property of the decedent that passes by intestate succession. If that individual or a member of that class survives the decedent, the share of the decedent's intestate estate to which that individual or class would have succeeded passes as if that individual or each member of that class had disclaimed his or her intestate share.

Michigan Compiled Laws, 700.2101

Share of spouse

1. The intestate share of a decedent's surviving spouse is one of the following:

   a. The entire intestate estate if no descendant or parent of the decedent survives the decedent.

   b. The first $150,000.00, plus 1/2 of any balance of the intestate estate, if all of the decedent's surviving descendants are also descendants of the surviving spouse and there is no other descendant of the surviving spouse who survives the decedent.

   c. The first $150,000.00, plus 3/4 of any balance of the intestate estate, if no descendant of the decedent survives the decedent, but a parent of the decedent survives the decedent.

   d. The first $150,000.00, plus 1/2 of any balance of the intestate estate, if all of the decedent's surviving descendants are also descendants of the surviving spouse and the surviving spouse has 1 or more surviving descendants who are not descendants of the decedent.

   e. The first $150,000.00, plus 1/2 of any balance of the intestate estate, if 1 or more, but not all, of the decedent's surviving descendants are not descendants of the surviving spouse.

   f. The first $100,000.00, plus 1/2 of any balance of the intestate estate, if none of the decedent's surviving descendants are descendants of the surviving spouse.

Each dollar amount listed in subsection (1) shall be adjusted as provided in section 1210.

Michigan Compiled Laws, 700.2102

Share of heirs other than surviving spouse

Any part of the intestate estate that does not pass to the decedent's surviving spouse under section 2102, or the entire intestate estate if there is no surviving spouse, passes in the following order to the following individuals who survive the decedent:

1. The decedent's descendants by representation.
2. If there is no surviving descendant, the decedent's parents equally if both survive or to the surviving parent.
3. If there is no surviving descendant or parent, the descendants of the decedent's parents or of either of them by representation.
4. If there is no surviving descendant, parent, or descendant of a parent, but the decedent is survived by 1 or more grandparents or descendants of grandparents, 1/2 of the estate passes to the decedent's paternal grandparents equally if both survive, or to the surviving paternal grandparent, or to the descendants of the decedent's paternal grandparents or either of them if both are deceased, the descendants taking by representation; and the other 1/2 passes to the decedent's maternal relatives in the same manner.

     If there is no surviving grandparent or descendant of a grandparent on either the paternal or the maternal side, the entire estate passes to the decedent's relatives on the other side in the same manner as the 1/2.

Michigan Compiled Laws, 700.2103

Requirement that heir survive decedent for 120 hours

An individual who fails to survive the decedent by 120 hours is considered to have predeceased the decedent for purposes of homestead allowance, exempt property, and intestate succession, and the decedent's heirs are determined accordingly. If it is not established by clear and convincing evidence that an individual who would otherwise be an heir survived the decedent by 120 hours, it is considered that the individual failed to survive for the required period. This section does not apply if its application would result in a taking of the intestate estate by the state under section 2105.

Michigan Compiled Laws, 700.2104

Disposition of estate if there is no taker

If there is no taker under the provisions of this article, the intestate estate passes to this state.

Michigan Compiled Laws, 700.2105

Sample Medical Power of Attorney and Advance Directive

Many states have approved forms for medical powers of attorney that are downloadable. Most of these forms are legal and usable in any other state as well. Using these eliminates the decision as to who should make your medical decisions if you can't do this yourself and so helps eliminate the need for a court-ordered guardianship through the probate court. Here is a link to the one Michigan uses: http://www.med.umich .edu/1libr/AdvanceDirectives/ADbooklet.pdf

The following is the text of the California Medical Power of Attorney as set out in state law to give you an idea as to how some of them are worded.

PROBATE CODE—PROB
DIVISION 4.7. HEALTH CARE DECISIONS [4600–4806]
(Division 4.7 added by Stats. 1999, Ch. 658, Sec. 39.)
PART 2. UNIFORM HEALTH CARE DECISIONS ACT [4670–4743]
(Part 2 added by Stats. 1999, Ch. 658, Sec. 39.)
CHAPTER 2. Advance Health Care Directive Forms [4700–4701]
(Chapter 2 added by Stats. 1999, Ch. 658, Sec. 39.)

4701.

The statutory advance health care directive form is as follows:

ADVANCE HEALTH CARE DIRECTIVE
(California Probate Code Section 4701)

Explanation

You have the right to give instructions about your own health care. You also have the right to name someone else to make health care decisions for you. This form lets you do either or both of these things. It also lets you express your wishes regarding donation of organs and the designation of your primary physician. If you use this form, you may complete or modify all or any part of it. You are free to use a different form.

Part 1 of this form is a power of attorney for health care. Part 1 lets you name another individual as agent to make health care decisions for you if you become incapable of making your own decisions or if you want someone else to make those decisions for you now even though you are still capable. You may also name an alternate agent to act for you if your first choice is not willing, able, or reasonably available to make decisions for you. (Your agent may not be an operator or employee of a community care facility or a residential care facility where you are receiving care, or your supervising health care provider or employee of the health care institution where you are receiving care, unless your agent is related to you or is a coworker.)

Unless the form you sign limits the authority of your agent, your agent may make all health care decisions for you. This form has a place for you to limit the authority of your agent. You need not limit the authority of your agent if you wish to rely on your agent for all health care decisions that may have to be made. If you choose not to limit the authority of your agent, your agent will have the right to:

a. Consent or refuse consent to any care, treatment, service, or procedure to maintain, diagnose, or otherwise affect a physical or mental condition.

b. Select or discharge health care providers and institutions.

c. Approve or disapprove diagnostic tests, surgical procedures, and programs of medication.

d. Direct the provision, withholding, or withdrawal of artificial nutrition and hydration and all other forms of health care, including cardiopulmonary resuscitation.

e. Donate your organs, tissues, and parts, authorize an autopsy, and direct disposition of remains.

Part 2 of this form lets you give specific instructions about any aspect of your health care, whether or not you appoint an agent. Choices are provided for you to express your wishes regarding the provision, withholding, or withdrawal of treatment to keep you alive, as well as the provision of pain relief. Space is also provided for you to add to the choices you have made or for you to write out any additional wishes. If you are satisfied to allow your agent to determine what is best for you in making end-of-life decisions, you need not fill out Part 2 of this form.

Part 3 of this form lets you express an intention to donate your bodily organs, tissues, and parts following your death.

Part 4 of this form lets you designate a physician to have primary responsibility for your health care.

After completing this form, sign and date the form at the end. The form must be signed by two qualified witnesses or acknowledged before a notary public. Give a copy of the signed and completed form to your physician, to any other health care providers you may have, to any health care institution at which you are receiving care, and to any health care agents you have named. You should talk to the person you have named as agent to make sure that he or she understands your wishes and is willing to take the responsibility.

You have the right to revoke this advance health care directive or replace this form at any time.

PART 1
POWER OF ATTORNEY FOR HEALTH CARE

(1.1) DESIGNATION OF AGENT. I designate the following:

_____

(Name of Individual)

_____

(Address)

_____

(City)   (State)   (Zip Code)

_____   _____

(Home Phone)   (Work Phone)

OPTIONAL: If I revoke my agent's authority or if my agent is not willing, able, or reasonably available to make a health care decision for me, I designate as my first alternate agent:

_____
(Name of Individual)

_____
(Address)

_____
(City)   (State)   (Zip Code)

_____   _____
(Home Phone)   (Work Phone)

OPTIONAL: If I revoke the authority of my agent and
first alternate agent or if neither is willing, able, or reasonably available to make a health care decision for me, I
designate as my second alternate agent:

_____
(Name of Individual)

_____
(Address)

_____
(City)   (State)   (Zip Code)

_____   _____
(Home Phone)   (Work Phone)

(1.2) AGENT'S AUTHORITY: My agent is authorized to make all health care decisions for me,
including decisions to provide, withhold, or withdraw artificial nutrition and hydration and all other
forms of health care to keep me alive, except as I
state here:

_____
_____
_____
_____
_____

(Add additional sheets if needed.)

(1.3) WHEN AGENT'S AUTHORITY BECOMES EFFECTIVE: My agent's authority becomes effective when my primary physician determines that I am unable to make my own health care decisions unless I mark the following box. If I mark this box ☐, my agent's authority to make health care decisions for me takes effect immediately.

(1.4) AGENT'S OBLIGATION: My agent shall make health care decisions for me in accordance with this power of attorney for health care, any instructions I give in Part 2 of this form, and my other wishes to the extent known to my agent. To the extent my wishes are unknown, my agent shall make health care decisions for me in accordance with what my agent determines to be in my best interest. In determining my best interest, my agent shall consider my personal values to the extent known to my agent.

(1.5) AGENT'S POSTDEATH AUTHORITY: My agent is authorized to donate my organs, tissues, and parts, authorize an autopsy, and direct disposition of my remains, except as I state here or in Part 3 of this form:

_____
_____
_____
_____
_____

(Add additional sheets if needed.)

(1.6) NOMINATION OF CONSERVATOR: If a conservator of my person needs to be appointed for me by a court, I nominate the agent designated in this form. If that agent is not willing, able, or reasonably available to act as conservator, I nominate the alternate agents whom I have named, in the order designated.

PART 2
INSTRUCTIONS FOR HEALTH CARE
(If you fill out this part of the form, you may strike any wording you do not want.)

(2.1) END-OF-LIFE DECISIONS: I direct that my health care providers and others involved in my care provide, withhold, or withdraw treatment in accordance with the choice I have marked below:

☐ (a) Choice Not to Prolong Life
I do not want my life to be prolonged if (1) I have an incurable and irreversible condition that will result in my death within a relatively short time, (2) I become unconscious and, to a reasonable degree of medical certainty, I will not regain consciousness, or (3) the likely risks and burdens of treatment would outweigh the expected benefits, OR

☐ (b) Choice to Prolong Life
I want my life to be prolonged as long as possible within the limits of generally accepted health care standards.

(2.2) RELIEF FROM PAIN: Except as I state in the following space, I direct that treatment for alleviation of pain or discomfort be provided at all times, even if it hastens my death:

_____

_____

_____

_____

_____

(Add additional sheets if needed.)

(2.3) OTHER WISHES: (If you do not agree with any
of the optional choices above and wish to write your
own, or if you wish to add to the instructions you
have given above, you may do so here.) I direct that:

_____

_____

_____

_____

_____

(Add additional sheets if needed.)

PART 3
DONATION OF ORGANS, TISSUES, AND PARTS AT DEATH (OPTIONAL)

☐ YES ☐ NO

(3.1) Upon my death, I give my organs, tissues, and parts
(mark box to indicate yes). By checking the box
above, and notwithstanding my choice in Part 2 of
this form, I authorize my agent to consent to any
temporary medical procedure necessary solely to
evaluate and/or maintain my organs, tissues, and/or
parts for purposes of donation.

My donation is for the following purposes (strike
any of the following you do not want):

a. Transplant
b. Therapy
c. Research
d. Education

(If you want to restrict your donation of an organ, tissue, or part in some way, please state your restriction on the following lines.)

_____

_____

_____

_____

_____

If I leave this part blank, it is not a refusal to make a dona-tion. My state-authorized donor registration should be followed, or, if none, my agent may make a donation upon my death. If no agent is named above, I acknowledge that California law permits an authorized individual to make such a decision on my behalf. (To state any limitation, preference, or instruction regarding donation, please use the lines above or in Section 1.5 of this form.)

PART 4
PRIMARY PHYSICIAN (OPTIONAL)

(4.1) I designate the following physician as my primary physician:

_____

(Name of Individual)

_____

(Address)

_____

(City)   (State)   (Zip Code)

_____

(Phone)

OPTIONAL: If the physician I have designated above is not willing, able, or reasonably available to act as my primary physician, I designate the following physician as my primary physician:

_____
(Name of Individual)

_____
(Address)

_____
(City)   (State)   (Zip Code)

_____
(Phone)

PART 5

(5.1) EFFECT OF COPY: A copy of this form has the same effect as the original.

(5.2) SIGNATURE: Sign and date the form here:

_____   _____
(Signature)   (Date)

_____
(Print Name)

_____
(Address)

_____
(City)   (State)   (Zip Code)

(5.3) STATEMENT OF WITNESSES: I declare under penalty of perjury under the laws of California (1) that the individual who signed or acknowledged this advance health care directive is personally known to me, or that the individual's identity was proven to me by convincing evidence, (2) that the individual signed or acknowledged this advance directive in my presence, (3) that the individual appears to be of sound mind and under no duress, fraud, or undue influence, (4) that I am not a person appointed as agent by this advance directive, and (5) that I am not the individual's health care provider, an employee of the individual's health care provider, the operator of a community care facility, an employee of an operator of a community care facility, the operator of a residential care facility for the elderly, nor an employee of an operator of a residential care facility for the elderly.

First Witness

_____   _____
(Signature of Witness)   (Date)

_____
(Print Name)

_____
(Address)

_____
(City)   (State)   (Zip Code)

Second Witness

_____   _____
(Signature of Witness)   (Date)

_____
(Print Name)

_____
(Address)

_____
(City)   (State)   (Zip Code)

(5.4) ADDITIONAL STATEMENT OF WITNESSES: At least one of the above witnesses must also sign the following declaration:

I further declare under penalty of perjury under the laws of California that I am not related to the individual executing this advance health care directive by blood, marriage, or adoption, and to the best of my knowledge, I am not entitled to any part of the individual's estate upon his or her death under a will now existing or by operation of law.

_____   _____
(Signature of First Witness)   (Date)

_____
(Print Name)

_____   _____
(Signature of Second Witness)   (Date)

_____
(Print Name)

PART 6
SPECIAL WITNESS REQUIREMENT

(6.1) The following statement is required only if you are a patient in a skilled nursing facility—a health care facility that provides the following basic services: skilled nursing care and supportive care to patients whose primary need is for availability of skilled nursing care on an extended basis. The patient advocate or ombudsman must sign the following statement:

STATEMENT OF PATIENT ADVOCATE OR OMBUDSMAN

I declare under penalty of perjury under the laws of California that I am a patient advocate or ombudsman as designated by the State Department of Aging and that I am serving as a witness as required by Section 4675 of the Probate Code.

_____   _____
(Signature of Special Witness)   (Date)

_____
(Print Name)

_____
(Address)

_____
(City)   (State)   (Zip Code)

(Amended by Stats. 2018, Ch. 287, Sec. 1. (AB 3211) Effective January 1, 2019.)

Sample Durable Springing Power of Attorney

This type of power of attorney takes effect if two physicians agree that you are unable to manage your own financial affairs due to physical or mental disability. By eliminating the italicized portion, it becomes just a durable power of attorney, which can be used by your agent to do all your business and sign your name while you are alive without the need for you to be incapacitated.

This power of attorney can be canceled, or a new agent can be named to act for you, any time you want by notifying the agent of the change. It's a good idea to notify your banker and investment people of the revocation or change in the agent's authority. This is one I have used and modified from time to time. Other attorneys use this form as well. It can be modified to include more or fewer powers as well as be limited in time. It might be that a power of attorney is prepared for only one specific act, such as selling a parcel of real estate. Our purpose for estate planning is to allow a named alternative agent of our choice rather than having a court appoint someone of their choice.

DURABLE POWER OF ATTORNEY

KNOW ALL MEN BY THESE PRESENTS, that I, _____,
SS# _____, residing at the following address ___ _____, hereby revoke any general power of attorney that I have heretofore given to any person, and by these Presents do constitute, make and appoint _____, my true and lawful attorney. If he/she is unable or unwilling or unable to serve as my agent, then I appoint _____ as my true and lawful attorney-in-fact and agent.

Until I am certified as incapacitated as provided hereunder, this Power of Attorney shall have no force or effect. All authority granted in this Power of Attorney shall be subject to establishment of incapacity as provided hereunder. After this Power of Attorney becomes effective, it shall not be affected by any subsequent incapacity which I may hereafter suffer or the passage of time. For purposes of establishing incapacity, whenever two licensed, practicing medical doctors who are not related to me or to any beneficiary or heir at law by blood or marriage certify in writing that I am unable to manage my financial affairs because of mental or physical infirmity and the certificates are personally served upon me, then the attorney(s)-in-fact named herein shall assume all powers granted in this Power of Attorney.

Anyone dealing with the attorney-in-fact may rely upon written medical certificates or a photocopy of them presented to them along with the original Power of Attorney document, and shall incur no liability for any dealings with any designated attorney(s)-in-fact in good faith reliance on said certificate and the original Power of Attorney document. This provision is inserted in this document to encourage third parties to deal with my attorney(s)-in-fact without the need for court proceedings.

By way of illustration, but not limitation, I specifically authorize my attorney to do the following:

1. To ask, demand, sue for, recover and receive all sums of money, debts, goods, merchandise, chattels, effects, and things of whatsoever nature or description which are now or hereafter shall be or become owing, due, payable, or belonging to me in or by any right whatsoever, and upon receipt thereof, to make, sign, execute, and deliver such receipts, releases, or other discharges for the same, respectively, as (s)he shall think fit.

2. To deposit any moneys which may come into his/her hands as such attorney with any bank or bankers, either in my or his/her own name, and any of such money or any other money to which I am entitled which now is or shall be so deposited to withdraw as (s)he shall think fit; to sign mutual savings bank and federal savings and loan association withdrawal orders; to sign and endorse checks payable to my order and to draw, accept, make, endorse, discount, or otherwise deal with any bills of exchange, checks, promissory notes, or other commercial or mercantile instruments; to borrow any sum or sums of money on such terms and with such security as he may think fit and for that purpose to execute all notes or other instruments which may be necessary or proper; and to have access to any and all safe deposit boxes registered in my name.

3. To sell, assign, transfer, and dispose of any and all stocks, bonds (including U.S. Savings Bonds), loans, mortgages, or other securities registered in my name; and to collect and receipt for all interest and dividends due and payable to me.

4. To invest in my name in any stock, shares, bonds (including U.S. Treasury Bonds referred to as "flower bonds"), securities, or other property, real or personal, and to vary such investments as (s)he, in his/her sole discretion, may deem best; and to vote at meetings of shareholders or other meetings of any corporation or company and to execute any proxies or other instruments in connection therewith.

5. To enter into and upon my real estate, and to let, manage, and improve the same or any part thereof, and to repair or otherwise improve or alter, and to insure any buildings thereon; to sell, either at public or private sale or exchange any part or parts of my real estate or personal property for such consideration and upon such terms as (s)he shall think fit, and to execute and deliver good and sufficient deeds or other instruments for the conveyance or transfer of the same, with such covenants of warranty or otherwise as (s)he shall see fit, and to give good and effectual receipts for all or any part of the purchase price or other consideration; and to mortgage my real estate and in connection therewith to execute bonds and warrants and all other necessary instruments and documents.

6. To contract with any person for leasing for such periods, at such rents and subject to such conditions as (s)he shall see fit, all or any of my said real estate; to give notice to quit to any tenant or occupier thereof; and to receive and recover from all tenants and occupiers thereof or of any part thereof all rents, arrears of rent, and sums of money which now are or shall hereafter become due and payable in respect thereof; and also on non-payment

thereof or of any part thereof, to take all necessary or proper means and proceedings for determining the tenancy or occupation of such tenants or occupiers, and for ejecting the tenants or occupiers and recovering the possession thereof.

7. To commence, prosecute, discontinue, or defend all actions or other legal proceedings pertaining to me or my estate or any part thereof, to settle, compromise, or submit to arbitration any debt, demand, or other right or matter due me or concerning my estate as (s)he, in his/her sole discretion, shall deem best and for such purpose to execute and deliver such releases, discharges, or other instruments as (s)he may deem necessary and advisable; and to satisfy mortgages, including the execution of a good and sufficient release, or other discharge of such mortgage.

8. To prepare and file all income and other federal and state tax returns which the principal is required to file; to sign the principal's name to tax returns; hire preparers and advisors and pay for their services; and to do whatever is necessary to protect the principal's assets from assessments for income taxes and other taxes. The agent is specifically authorized to receive confidential information; to receive checks in payment of any refund of taxes, penalties, or interest; to execute waivers (including offers of waivers) of restrictions on assessment or collection of tax deficiencies and waivers of notice of disallowance of claims for credit or refund; to execute consents extending the statutory period for assessment or collection claims for credit or credit refund; to execute closing agreements under Internal Revenue Code section 7121,

or any successor statute; and to delegate authority or substitute another representative with respect to all above matters.

9. To engage, employ, and dismiss any agents, clerks, servants, or other persons as (s)he, in his/her sole discretion, shall deem necessary and advisable.

10. To convey and transfer any of my property to trustees who shall hold the same for my benefit and/or the benefit of my children and other members of my immediate family upon such trust terms and conditions as my attorney(s)-in-fact shall deem desirable.

11. To make gifts on the principal's behalf to a class composed of the principal's children, any of their issue, or both, to the full extent of the federal annual gift tax exclusion in effect from time to time, including the annual exclusion under Internal Revenue Code section 2503(b) or any successor statute, and for such purposes to remove the principal's assets from any grantor's revocable trust of which the principal is a grantor.

12. To disclaim any interest in property for the purpose of making a qualified disclaimer within the meaning of section 2518 of the Internal Revenue Code.

13. To have access to all safe deposit boxes in the principal's name or to which the principal is an authorized signatory; to contract with financial institutions for the maintenance and continuation of safe deposit boxes in the principal's name; to add to and remove the contents of all such safe deposit boxes; and to terminate contracts for all such safe deposit boxes.

14. To use any credit cards in the principal's name to make purchases and to sign charge slips on behalf

of the principal as may be required to use such credit cards; and to close the principal's charge accounts and terminate the principal's credit cards under circumstances where the agent considers such acts to be in the principal's best interest.

15. In general, to do all other acts, deeds, and matters whatsoever in or about my estate, property, and affairs as fully and effectually to all intents and purposes as I could do in my own proper person if personally present, giving to my said attorney power to make and substitute under him/her an attorney or attorneys for all the purposes herein described, hereby ratifying and confirming all that the said attorney or substitute or substitutes shall do therein by virtue of these Presents.

16. In addition to the powers and discretion herein specially given and conferred upon my attorney, and notwithstanding any usage or custom to the contrary, to have the full power, right, and authority to do, perform, and to cause to be done and performed all such acts, deeds, and matters in connection with my property and estate as (s)he, in his/her sole discretion, shall deem reasonable, necessary and proper, as fully, effectually, and absolutely as if he were the absolute owner and possessor thereof.

17. My agent may not execute any trust instrument, or any document connected with the creation of a trust, or the amendment, modification, revocation (in whole or in part), or termination of an existing trust instrument to which I am a party.

IN WITNESS HEREOF I have signed my name this
_____ day of _____ 20_____.

_____
(Signature)

Witnessed:

_____   _____
(Signature)   (Signature)

_____   _____
(Print Name)   (Print Name)

STATE OF _____

COUNTY OF _____

On this _____ day of _____
20_____: Before me a Notary Public personally
appeared _____ (*sign-ee's name*) known to me to be the person whose name is subscribed to this instrument who provided proper identification and acknowledged that he executed it for the purposes herein expressed.

_____
(Notary Public Signature)

(Seal)

Sample Information Form to Take to Your Attorney to Start the Trust Process

CONFIDENTIAL INFORMATION FORM

YOUR NAME: Mr./Mrs./Ms. _____

U.S. Citizen? Yes _____ No _____

Date of Birth: _____

SPOUSE'S NAME: Mr./Mrs./Ms._____

U.S. Citizen? Yes _____ No _____

Date of Birth: _____

Telephone: _____

_____

(Street Address)

_____

(City) (State) (Zip Code)

_____

(Mailing Address—if different from above)

_____

(City) (State) (Zip Code)

Children (Including those deceased)

Name: _____

DOB: ____ / ____ / ____ Living? Yes____ No____

Name: _____

DOB: ____ / ____ / ____ Living? Yes____ No____

Name: _____

DOB: ____ / ____ / ____ Living? Yes____ No____

Name: _____

DOB: ____ / ____ / ____ Living? Yes____ No____

Name:_____

DOB: ____ / ____ / ____ Living? Yes____ No____

Name:_____

DOB: ____ / ____ / ____ Living? Yes____ No____

Are any children either disabled, under a court ordered guardianship, or receiving governmental assistance such as Medicaid? If so, explain:

_____

_____

_____

_____

_____

Who do you want to handle your estate after your death? Spouse first? Yes____ No____

In the following Order? _____ or Jointly? _____
(1)
Name: _____

Relationship to you: _____

Telephone:_____

Address: _____

_____

(2)
Name: _____

Relationship to you: _____

Telephone:_____

Address: _____

_____

(3)
Name: _____

Relationship to you: _____

Telephone:_____

Address: _____

_____

To whom are you leaving your assets? (If a charity or church, also give address.) *If you want to structure a distribution to a beneficiary (for example paying it out in installments or at a certain age), please attach a separate sheet with those instructions.*

Name: _____ %:_____

Name: _____ %:_____

Name: _____ %:_____

Name: _____ %:_____

Name: _____ %:_____

Name: _____ %:_____

Who do you want to make medical decisions for you if you are unable to do so for yourself?
Your choices:
1. _____
2. Alternate: _____
3. Second Alternate: _____

Your spouse's choices:
1. _____
2. Alternate: _____
3. Second Alternate: _____

Sample Simple Trust

The following is a sample of a revocable living trust for a married couple with two minor children in a non-community property state. This is presented here so you can get an idea of what a trust looks like.

THIS IS NOT A TRUST THAT YOU SHOULD COPY AND USE.

Trusts are set up for particular purposes and no two are exactly alike. Your personal financial and family situation as well as your wishes on things such as guardianship, distribution of trust assets, restrictions on beneficiaries' use of funds, and many other issues need to be covered by the trust document terms. This particular sample is one I have used and modified over the years and in fact has been copied and used by other attorneys, but you need to have yours drafted based on your situation. There is no one-size-fits-all trust.

Trust funding documents are also not included here since they vary from state to state and institution to institution.

SUMMARY OF TRUST PROVISIONS

Grantor Name: John H. Doe
Grantor Residence Address at Time of Signing: 1234
  Elm Street, Anytown, Michigan
State Law Governing the Trust (Situs): Michigan
Name of Trust: The John H. Doe Revocable Trust dated
  April 1, 2021
Date Signed: April 1, 2021
Initial Trustee: John H. Doe
**Name of Successor Trustee on Death or Disability of
  Grantor:** Kevin I. Doe
  Address: 1221 North Main Street, Detroit, MI
Alternate Successor Trustee: Judith Doe-Jones
  Address: 1900 Happy Valley, San Diego, CA

Powers of Grantor as Trustee
  Section 6 Page 12, et seq
Powers of Successor Trustee at Disability of Grantor
  Section 7 Page 16
Powers of Successor Trustee at Death of Grantor
  Section 7 Page 17 et seq
Distribution of Trust Assets at the Death of Grantor
  Section 8 Page 22
Distribution of Personal Property at Death of Grantor
  Appendix 1 Page 31
Amendments to Trust
  Appendix 2 Page 32

*Note that this summary is not a part of the trust document but
merely a reference tool for accessing the document language.*

The John Doe and Jane Doe

Revocable Living Trust Agreement

Dated: _____

BETWEEN: John Doe and Jane Doe,
AS GRANTORS

AND: John Doe and Jane Doe,
AS TRUSTEES

John Doe and Jane Doe, who reside at 1234 Elm Street, Ann Arbor, Michigan, ZIP, do hereby establish a Trust upon the conditions and for the purposes hereafter set forth.

ARTICLE ONE

Section 1.01. Trust Estate Defined

This Revocable Trust is formed to hold title to real and personal property for the benefit of the Grantors of this Trust and to provide for the orderly use and transfer of these assets upon the death of the Grantors. The "Trust Estate" is defined as all property, transferred or conveyed to and received by the Trustee, held pursuant to the terms of this instrument. The Trustee is required to hold, administer, and distribute this property as provided in this Trust Agreement.

Section 1.02. Definitions

As used in this Trust Agreement,

   a. The term "husband" shall mean John Doe.
   b. The term "wife" shall mean Jane Doe.
   c. The term "Grantor" shall refer individually and collectively to husband and wife.

d. The term "descendant" shall mean the lawful issue of a deceased parent in the line of descent but does not include the issue of any parent who is a descendant of the deceased person in question and is living at the time in question.

e. The terms "child" and "descendant" include any issue born to decedent or legally adopted by the decedent or a posthumous child of a decedent, and a posthumous child is to be considered as living at the time of his or her parent's death.

f. The term "survives" or "surviving," unless otherwise indicated herein, shall be construed to mean surviving the decedent for at least sixty (60) days. If the person referred to dies within sixty (60) days of the death of the decedent, the reference to him or her will be construed as if he or she had failed to survive the decedent; provided, however, that any such person will have during such period the right to the use and the enjoyment as a life tenant of all property in which his or her interest will fail by reason of death during such period.

g. The term "issue" will include all natural and adopted children, if applicable, and descendants and those legally adopted into the line of descent.

h. The term "per stirpes" means strict per stirpes and does not mean per capita with representation. Beneficiaries entitled to take under a "per stirpes" clause will include both natural and adopted children and their descendants.

i. The terms "Trust Assets" and "Trust Estate" include all assets of any trust created hereunder and income derived from such assets and all proceeds of any description derived from the sale, exchange, or other disposition of such assets.

j. When required to give reasonable effect to the context in which used, pronouns in the masculine, feminine, or neutral gender include each other, and nouns and pronouns in the plural or singular number include each other.

Section 1.03. Trustee Designation

Husband and wife are hereby designated as Co-Trustees. The Co-Trustees shall serve jointly and neither shall have full authority to act for the Trust independently. Should either husband or wife become unable because of death, incapacity, or other cause to serve as a Co-Trustee, or should either resign as Co-Trustee before the natural termination of this Trust, the remaining Co-Trustee, husband or wife, shall thereafter serve as sole Trustee. Co-Trustees can agree to appoint by power of attorney the other Trustee to act for him or her regarding specific actions or transactions of the Trust.

Section 1.04. Additions to Trust Properties

a. The Trustee, at any time during the continuance of this Trust, in his or her sole discretion after consideration of the possible tax consequences to all concerned, is authorized to receive into the Trust additions of cash and other properties from any source whatsoever, whether by gift, will, or otherwise. However, the Trustee shall accept all assets which any person or persons may give, devise, or bequeath by Last Will and Testament to this Trust, and shall accept all assets transferred to this Trust pursuant to the provisions of any other Trust document or documents. The Trustee does retain the right to disclaim assets if in the interests of the Trust Estate.

b. In addition, any person or persons may designate this Trust as the Beneficiary, Primary or Contingent, of death benefits, whether insurance benefits, pension benefits, or other benefits. Until such benefits mature, the Trustee shall have no responsibility with respect to those benefits.

Section 1.05. Apportionment

The Trustee of the Trust is directed to apportion receipts and expenditures of the types described below between principal and income as follows:

a. Whenever the principal, or any part thereof, of the Trust property is invested in securities purchased at a premium or at a discount, any premium will be charged against principal and any discount will be credited to principal;

b. Any stock dividends and rights to purchase additional stock issued on securities held in trust will be treated as principal, but all other dividends, except liquidating distributions, will be treated as income; and

c. The amount of any applicable depletion allowance for federal income tax purposes will be treated as income.

Section 1.06. Administration of Trust During Grantors' Lifetimes

During grantors' lifetimes, the Trust Estate shall be held and administered as follows:

1. All property and other assets transferred to this Trust shall be held in the name of the Trust and not in separate shares. The Trustees shall hold and manage the Trust assets for the use and benefit of the Grantors during their lifetimes. The Trustee shall pay to or apply for the benefit of Grantors all of the net income of the Trust, in convenient installments, not less often than quarter-annually, and in

addition thereto shall pay so much of the income and principal of such Trust share to or for the benefit of Grantors, as they may direct from time to time, or in the absence of a direction, as the Trustee may determine to be advisable for their medical care, support, maintenance, and general welfare.

2. If the Grantors are acting as their own Trustees, they retain an unrestricted right to the use and management of all Trust assets for their own benefit or for the benefit of others as they shall decide.

Section 1.07. Discretionary Termination

The Trustee may terminate any Trust when, in the opinion of the Trustee, the principal is reduced to such an extent that it is not in the best interest of the Beneficiary or Beneficiaries to continue the Trust. The judgment of the Trustee with respect to this decision to terminate will be final and not subject to judicial review. If the Trustee terminates a Trust according to this Section, the date the Trust terminates will be deemed the date fixed for termination of the Trust, and the Trustee will distribute the assets of the terminating Trust to the Beneficiary or Beneficiaries pursuant to this Agreement.

Section 1.08. Amendment and Revocation

Grantors hereby retain the following joint powers, exercisable by their joint action at any time during their lifetimes:

1. To withdraw, sell, invest, transfer, or encumber any of the property included in the Trust Estate.
2. To amend the provisions of this Trust declaration in any respect.
3. To revoke this Trust.

At the death or disability of one Grantor before the other, the survivor shall continue to act as Trustee and shall have the right to amend the Trust, but shall not be able to amend it in such a way as to reduce the previous pro rata monetary share of the children of the other Grantor; nor shall the survivor have the power to remove assets from this Trust ownership if such removal acts to effectively reduce the share to those children. This provision does not, however, affect the right of the survivor to use the Trust assets for his or her own support and the beneficiaries shall have no right to supervise or approve any normal expenditure of the survivor, recognizing that the primary use of Trust assets is for the benefit of the Grantors during their lifetimes.

Section 1.09. Revocation or Alteration by Grantor Alone

The rights of revocation, withdrawal, alteration, and amendment reserved in this Article must be exercised by the Grantor, the surviving Grantor, or a Successor Trustee acting for a Grantor in a fiduciary capacity during the Grantor's lifetime, and may not be exercised by any other person, including an agent, a guardian, or a conservator.

Section 1.10. Irrevocability

Except as otherwise provided, on the death of either Grantor, the designation of Beneficiaries of specific gifts in this Trust on Exhibit A shall become irrevocable, and not subject to amendment or modification; however, the surviving Grantor retains the right to amend the Trust in all other respects.

Section 1.11. Grantor Powers

The surviving Grantor shall be the Trustee unless and until he or she resigns in writing, or is determined incompetent under the terms provided herein. The surviving

Grantor shall retain all absolute rights to discharge or replace any successor Trustee of any portion or share of the Trust which is revocable by the surviving Grantor, so long as the Grantor is competent.

ARTICLE TWO

Section 2.01. Trust Income

During the joint lives of the Grantors, the Trustee shall at least annually, unless otherwise directed by both Grantors in writing, pay to or apply for the benefit of husband and wife, all of the net income from the Trust Estate.

Section 2.02. Protection of Grantor in Event of Incapacity

During the joint lives of the Grantors, should either Grantor become incapacitated as defined in Section 2.03 below, the Trustee may, in the Trustee's absolute discretion, pay income and principal for the benefit of the incapacitated Grantor, and may pay to or apply for the benefit of that Grantor such sums from the net income and from the principal of the Grantor's separate Estate as the Trustee, in the Trustee's absolute discretion, believes is necessary or advisable for the medical care, comfortable maintenance, and welfare of the Grantor.

Section 2.03. Incapacity

In the event that any Trustee or any Beneficiary hereunder comes into possession of any of the following:

a. A jurisdictionally applicable court order holding the party to be legally incapacitated to act on his or her own behalf and appointing a guardian or conservator to act for him or her, or

b. Written certificates which are duly executed, witnessed, and acknowledged of two licensed physicians, each certifying that the physician has examined the person and has concluded that, by reason of accident, mental deterioration, or other cause, such person has become incapacitated and can no longer act rationally and prudently in his or her own financial best interests, or

c. Evidence which such Trustee or Beneficiary deems to be credible and currently applicable that a person has disappeared, is unaccountably absent, or is being detained under duress, and that he or she is unable to effectively and prudently look after his or her own best interests, then in that event and under those circumstances:

    a. Such person is deemed to have become incapacitated, as that term is used in this Trust Agreement, and

    b. Such incapacity is deemed to continue until such court order, certificates, and/or circumstances are inapplicable or have been revoked.

A physician's certificate to the effect that the person is no longer incapacitated shall revoke a certificate declaring the person incapacitated. The certificate which revokes the earlier certificate may be executed either (1) by the originally certifying physician or (2) by two other licensed, board certified physicians. No Trustee shall be under any duty to institute any inquiry into a person's possible incapacity. The reasonable expense of any such inquiry shall be paid from the Trust Assets.

Section 2.04. Principal Invasion

During the joint lives of the Grantors, should the net income of assets contained in this Trust be insufficient to provide for the care, maintenance, or support of the

Grantors as herein defined, the Trustee may, in the Trustee's sole and absolute discretion, pay to or apply for the benefit of the Grantors or either of them, or any of their dependents, such amounts from the principal of the Trust Estate as the Trustee deems necessary or advisable for the care, maintenance, or support of the Grantors.

Section 2.05. Residence

If the Grantors' residence property is a part of the Trust, the Grantors shall have possession of and full management of the residence and shall have the right to occupy it rent-free. Any expenses arising from the maintenance of the property and from all taxes, liens, assessments, and insurance premiums are to be paid from the Trust to the extent that assets are available for payment. It is the intent of the Grantors to retain all homestead rights available to them under the applicable state law.

ARTICLE THREE

Section 3.01. Administration on Grantors' Deaths

At the death of one Grantor the Trust shall continue and the surviving Grantor shall be the sole Trustee with full power and authority to revoke, amend, or change the Trust in any way and shall be in full control and have use of all Trust assets. After the death of both Grantors the Trust shall be distributed according to the provisions of Article Four, but the Successor Trustee(s) shall have no authority to amend the terms of this Trust or change the distribution as set out in Article Four, except as may be necessary for tax saving purposes.

ARTICLE FOUR

Section 4.01. Common Pot Trust

At the death of the Surviving Grantor, our Trustee may create a Common Pot Trust. All of our Trust Estate that has not been distributed under prior Articles of our Trust Agreement shall be held, administered, divided, and distributed according to the provisions that follow.

Section 4.02. Second Death

On the death of the last Grantor to die (the "Surviving Grantor"), the Trustee shall distribute the principal of the Trust and any accrued or undistributed income from the principal of the Trust in such a manner and to such persons, including the Estate or the Creditors, as directed in this Trust Agreement.

Section 4.03. Payment of the Second Death Expenses

On the death of the surviving Grantor, the Trustee shall pay from that portion of the trust estate constituting the deceased Grantor's separate Trust share the expenses of the surviving Grantor's last illness, funeral, burial, and any inheritance, estate, or death taxes that may be due by reason of the surviving Grantor's death, unless the Trustee in his or her absolute discretion determines that other adequate provisions have been made for the payment of such expenses and taxes.

Section 4.04. Trust Income and Principal Distribution Upon the Death of the Surviving Grantor

a. The Trustee shall apply and distribute the net income and principal of the Trust Estate (after giving effect to the section of this Trust Agreement entitled "Special Directives") to the following Beneficiaries in the indicated fractional shares:

One-half to Billie Jean Doe and one-half to Robert F. Doe, our children.

b. If any Beneficiary (including but not limited to a grandchild if any) is under the age of 25 years when the distribution is to be made, the Trustee shall retain any such property and administer and distribute the same for the benefit of the Beneficiary, paying to or for the benefit of such person so much of the income and principal of the retained property from time to time, as the Trustee deems advisable for his or her health, education, support, and maintenance. When the person for whom the property is held attains the age of 25 years, the property shall thereupon be distributed to him or her free of trust. If the person should die before attaining the age of 25, the property shall then be paid and distributed to the estate of the person.

c. If all of the Grantor's Beneficiaries and their children should fail to survive the final distribution of the Trust Estate, all of the Trust Estate not disposed of as hereinabove provided shall be distributed one-half to the heirs at law of each Grantor.

Section 4.05. Principle of Representation

Unless indicated differently in this Trust Agreement or in the "SPECIAL DIRECTIVES" section that follows, in the event any of Grantors' named Beneficiaries should predecease both of them, all of that person's share of the Trust Estate is to be divided equally among the deceased Beneficiary's children or issue per stirpes. In the event the predeceased Beneficiary leaves no surviving children or issue, then all of that person's share of the Trust Estate shall be divided equally among the remaining Beneficiaries per stirpes.

If a Beneficiary of the Grantors survives both Grantors, but should fail to survive to collect his or her share at distribution, that share shall pass to the surviving issue of that deceased Beneficiary per stirpes and with right of representation.

ARTICLE FIVE
Section 5.01. Non-Income Producing Property

During the joint lives of the Grantors, the Trustee is authorized to retain in the Trust, for so long as the Trustee may deem advisable, any property received by the Trustee from the Grantors, whether or not such property is of the character permitted by law for the investment of Trust funds and subject to the applicable restrictions of the Michigan Prudent Investor Rule.

Section 5.02. Trustee Powers

The Trustee shall have all powers conferred upon a Trustee by law for the orderly administration of the Trust Estate. If any property is distributed outright under the provision of this Trust Agreement to a person who is a minor, distribution may be made under the Michigan Uniform Gift to Minors Act ("MUGMA"). The Trustee is further authorized to sign, deliver, and/or receive any documents necessary to carry out the powers contained within this Section.

The Trustee of any trust created under this Trust Agreement (including any Substitute or Successor Trustee) will have and be subject to all of the powers, duties, and responsibilities granted or imposed by the Michigan, MCL 700.1, a *seq.*, as such Statute may provide at the time of administration of the Trust, except to the extent that the same are inconsistent with the provisions of this Agreement.

Any Trustee/Grantor has the power and authority to manage and control, buy, sell, and transfer the Trust property, in such manner as the Trustee may deem advisable, and shall have, enjoy, and exercise all powers and rights over and concerning said property and the proceeds thereof as fully and amply as though said Trustee were the absolute and qualified owner of same, including the power to grant, bargain, sell and convey, encumber and hypothecate real and personal property, and the power to invest in corporate obligations of every kind, stocks, preferred or common, and to buy stocks, bonds, and similar investments on margin or other leveraged accounts, except to the extent that such management would cause includability of an irrevocable trust in the Estate of a Trustee.

Section 5.03. Specific Powers of Trustee
In addition, the Trustee will have the following specific powers:

a. Trust Estate—The Trustee may leave invested any property coming into its hands hereunder in any form of investment, even though the investment may not be of the character of investments permitted by law to Trustees, without liability for loss or depreciation in value. The Trustee may sell, exchange, or otherwise dispose of and reinvest property which may at any time be a part of the Trust Estate upon such terms and conditions as the Trustee may deem advisable. The Trustee may invest and reinvest the Trust Assets from time to time in any property, real, personal, or mixed, including without limitation securities of domestic and foreign corporations and investment trusts or companies, bonds, debentures, preferred stocks, common stocks, mortgages, mortgage participations, and interests in common trust funds, all with complete discretion to convert realty into personalty or personalty into realty or otherwise change the character of the Trust Estate, even though such investment (by reason of its character, amount, proportion to the total Trust Estate, or otherwise) would not be considered appropriate for a fiduciary apart from this provision, and even though such investment caused part or all of the total Trust Estate to be invested in investments of one type or of one business or company.

b. Holding Property—The Trustee may hold property in the Trustee's name, as trustee, or in the name of a nominee without disclosing the Trust.

c. Release of Power—If the Trustee deems it to be in the best interest of the Trust and its beneficiaries, the Trustee, by written instrument signed by such Trustee, will have the power and authority to release, disclaim, or restrict the scope of any power or discretion granted in this Trust Agreement or implied by law.

d. Agents, Employees—The Trustee may employ one or more agents to perform any act of administration, whether or not discretionary, including attorneys, auditors, investment managers, or others, as the Trustee shall deem necessary or advisable. The Trustee may compensate agents and other employees, and may delegate to them any and all discretions and powers.

e. Leases—The Trustee may lease any Trust Assets generally or for oil, gas, and mineral development, even though the lease term may extend beyond the term of the Trust of which the property is a part. The Trustee may enter into any covenants and agreements relating to the property so leased or any improvements which may then or thereafter be erected on such property.

f. Common Funds—The Trustee may hold any of the Trust Assets in a common fund with property from other trust estates and make investments jointly with any other trust, the property of which is included in the common fund.

g. Securities—With respect to securities held in the Trust Estate, the Trustee may exercise all the rights, powers, and privileges of an owner, including, but not limited to, the power to vote, to give proxies, and to pay assessments and other sums deemed by the Trustee necessary for the protection of the Trust estate; to participate in voting trusts, foreclosures, reorganizations, consolidations, mergers, and liquidations, and in connection therewith to deposit securities with and transfer title to any protective or other committee under such terms as the Trustee may deem advisable; to exercise or sell stock subscription or conversion rights; and to accept and retain as an investment any securities or other property received through the exercise of any of the foregoing powers, regardless of any limitations elsewhere in this instrument relative to investments by the Trustee.

h. Purchases from Estate—The Trustee may purchase property of any kind from the Personal Representative or administrator of our estates.

i. Lending—The Trustee may make loans, secured or unsecured, to the Personal Representative or administrator of our estates, to any beneficiary of the Trust or to the Trustee. Further, the Trustee may use Trust assets to guarantee obligations of any income beneficiary of the Trust (unless such beneficiary is serving as trustee).

j. Distributions to or for Beneficiaries—The Trustee may make any distribution contemplated by this Trust Agreement (1) to the Beneficiary, or (2) if the Beneficiary is under a legal disability or if the Trustee determines that the Beneficiary is unable to properly manage his or her affairs, to a person furnishing support, maintenance, or education for the Beneficiary or with whom the Beneficiary is residing, for expenditures on the Beneficiary's behalf, or (3) if the Beneficiary is a minor, to a trustee of an existing trust established exclusively for the benefit of such minor, whether created by this Trust Agreement or otherwise, or to a custodian for the Beneficiary, as selected by the Trustee, under the Michigan Uniform Gifts to Minors Act. Alternatively, the Trustee may apply all or a part of the distribution for the Beneficiary's benefit. Any distribution under this paragraph will be a full discharge of the Trustee with respect thereto. On any partial or final distribution of the Trust Assets, the Trustee may apportion and allocate the assets of the Trust Estate in cash or in kind, or partly in cash and partly in kind, or in undivided interests in the manner deemed advisable at the discretion of the Trustee and to sell any property deemed necessary by the Trustee to make the distribution. The Trustee may distribute gifts of up to the annual IRS exclusion amount per year per donee out of principal or interest.

k. Insurance—The Trustee may purchase new life insurance and pay the premiums on existing life insurance on the life of any Trust Beneficiary and may purchase annuities (either commercial or private) from any corporation, trust or individual; and may procure and pay the premiums on other insurance of the kinds, forms, and amounts deemed advisable by the Trustee to protect the Trustee and the Trust Estate.

l.   Borrowing—The Trustee may borrow money from the Trustee and others, and to secure the repayment thereof by mortgaging or pledging or otherwise encumbering any part or all of the Trust assets and, in connection with the acquisition of any property, may assume a liability or acquire property subject to a liability.

m.   Repairs—The Trustee may make ordinary and extraordinary repairs and alterations in buildings or other Trust Assets.

n.   Reserves—The Trustee may establish such reserves out of income for taxes, assessments, repairs, and maintenance as the Trustee considers appropriate.

o.   Continuation of Business—The Trustee may continue any business or businesses in which Grantors have an interest at the time of their death for so long as the Trustee may, in its sole discretion, consider necessary or desirable, whether or not the business is conducted by them at the time of their death individually, as a partnership, or as a corporation wholly owned or controlled by them, with full authority to sell, settle, and discontinue any of them when and upon such terms and conditions as the Trustee may, in its sole discretion, consider necessary or desirable.

p.   Retain Property for Personal Use—The trustee may retain a residence or other property for the personal use of a Beneficiary and to allow a Beneficiary to use or occupy the retained property free of rent and maintenance expenses.

q.   Dealings with Third Parties—The Trustee may deal with any person or entity regardless of relationship or identity of any Trustee to or with that person or entity and may hold or invest all or any part of the Trust Estate in common or undivided interests with that person or entity.

r. Partitions, Divisions, Distributions—The Trustee will have the power to make all partitions, divisions, and distributions contemplated by this Trust Agreement. Any partitions, divisions, or distributions may be made in cash, in kind, or partly in cash and partly in kind, in any manner that the Trustee deems appropriate (including composing shares differently). The Trustee may determine the value of any property, which valuation will be binding on all beneficiaries. No adjustments are required to compensate for any partitions, divisions, or distributions having unequal consequences to the beneficiaries.

s. Claims, Controversies—The Trustee may maintain and defend any claim or controversy by or against the Trust without the joinder or consent of any Beneficiary. The Trustee may commence or defend at the expense of the Trust any litigation with respect to the trust or any property of the Trust Estate as the Trustee may deem advisable, and may employ, for reasonable compensation, such counsel as the Trustee shall deem advisable for that purpose.

t. Merger of Trusts—If at any time the Trustee of any Trust created hereunder shall also be acting as trustee of any other trust created by trust instrument or by trust declaration for the benefit of the same Beneficiary or Beneficiaries and upon substantially the same terms and conditions, the Trustee is authorized and empowered, if in the Trustee's discretion such action is in the best interest of the Beneficiary or Beneficiaries, to transfer and merge all of the assets then held under such Trust created pursuant to this Trust Agreement to and with such other trust and thereupon to terminate the Trust created pursuant to this Trust Agreement. The Trustee is further authorized to accept the assets of any other trust which may be transferred to any Trust created hereunder and to administer and distribute such assets and properties so transferred in accordance with the provisions of this Agreement.

u. Termination of Small Trust—Any corporate Trustee which is serving as the sole Trustee of any Trust or any share thereof may at any time terminate such Trust or share if, in the Trustee's sole judgment, the continued management of such Trust or share is no longer economical because of the small size of such Trust or share and if such action will be deemed to be in the best interests of the Beneficiary or Beneficiaries. In case of such termination, the Trustee will distribute forthwith the share of the Trust Estate so terminated to the income Beneficiary or Beneficiaries, per stirpes. Upon such distribution, such Trust or share will terminate and the Trustee will not be liable or responsible to any person or persons whomsoever for its action. The Trustee will not be liable for failing or refusing at any time to terminate any Trust or a share thereof as authorized by this paragraph.

v. Power to Determine Income and Principal— Dividends payable in stock of the issuing corporation, stock splits, and capital gains will be treated as principal. Except as herein otherwise specifically provided, the Trustee will have full power and authority to determine the manner in which expenses are to be borne and in which receipts are to be credited as between principal and income, and also to determine what will constitute principal or income, and may withhold from income such reserves for depreciation or depletion as the Trustee may deem fair and equitable. In determining such matters the Trustee may give consideration to the provisions of the Michigan Statutes (or its successor statutes) relating to such matters, but will not be bound by such provisions.

w. Generation-Skipping Taxes and Payment—If the Trustee considers any distribution or termination of an interest or power hereunder as a distribution or termination subject to a generation-skipping tax, the Trustee is authorized:

1. To augment any taxable distribution by an amount which the Trustee estimates to be sufficient to pay such tax and charge the same to the particular Trust to which the tax related without adjustment of the relative interests of the Beneficiaries;

2. To pay such tax, in the case of a taxable termination, from the particular Trust to which the tax relates without adjustment of the relative interests of the Beneficiaries. If such tax is imposed in part by reason of the Trust Assets, the Trustee will pay only the portion of such tax attributable to the taxable termination hereunder taking into consideration deductions, exemptions, credits, and other factors which the Trustee deems advisable; and

3. To postpone final termination of any particular Trust and to withhold all or any portion of the Trust Estate until the Trustee is satisfied that the Trustee no longer has any liability to pay any generation-skipping tax with reference to such trust or its termination.

x. Partial distributions to trust beneficiaries—After the death of Grantors, the Trustee shall have the authority, in his or her absolute discretion, to make partial distributions of Trust Assets to the Beneficiaries named in this Trust on a pro rata basis, prior to the complete distribution of the Trust Assets according to its terms. The Trustee shall also have the authority to retain in the name of the Trust a portion of the Trust Assets for contemplated expenses during the interim between the death of the Grantors and final distribution.

Section 5.04. Special Provision for S Corporation Stock Notwithstanding what is otherwise provided in this Trust Agreement, if at any time the Trust contains any stock of a corporation which elects or has elected treatment as an "S Corporation" as defined by Section 1361 (a)(2)(D) of the Internal Revenue Code (or any corresponding successor statute), such stock will be segregated from the other assets of such Trust and treated as a separate trust. The Trustee will further divide the separate trust into shares for each Beneficiary and such shares will be distributed outright or held in trust as herein provided. In addition, all other provisions of this Trust Agreement will apply to each share held in trust (and constituting a separate trust) except that the Trustee will distribute all of the income from each separate trust to its Beneficiary in convenient installments at least annually. It is our intent that each separate trust will be recognized as a "Qualified Subchapter S Trust" (QSST) under Section 1361(d)(2) of the Internal Revenue Code (or any corresponding successor statute). Notwithstanding any provisions of this Trust Agreement to the contrary, the Trustee's powers and discretions with respect to the administration of each separate trust (including methods of accounting, bookkeeping, making distributions, and characterizing receipts and expenses) will not be exercised or exercisable except in a manner consistent with allowing each separate trust to be treated as a QSST as above described.

ARTICLE SIX
Section 6.01. Coordination with Grantor's Probate Estate

a. At any time during the continuance of this Trust including subsequent to the death of either Grantor the Trustees may, in their sole and uncontrolled discretion, distribute to the deceased Grantor's Probate Estate cash and/or other property as a Beneficiary of the Trust.

b. All other provisions to the contrary notwithstanding, under no circumstances shall any restricted proceeds, as hereinafter defined, be either directly or indirectly: (1) distributed to or for the benefit of the Grantor's Personal Representatives or the Grantor's Probate Estate; or (2) used to pay any other obligations of the Grantor's Estate. The term "restricted proceeds" means:

c. All qualified plans, individual retirement accounts, or similar benefits which are received or receivable by any Trustee hereunder, and which are paid solely to a Beneficiary other than the Personal Representative of the Grantor's Gross Estate for Federal Estate Tax purposes; and

d. All proceeds of insurance on the Grantor's life which, if paid to a Beneficiary other than the Grantor's Estate, would be exempt from inheritance or similar death taxes under applicable state death tax laws.

Section 6.02. Direction to Minimize Taxes

In the administration of the Trust hereunder, its Fiduciaries shall exercise all available tax-related elections, options, and choices in such a manner as they, in their sole but reasonable judgment (where appropriate, receiving advice of tax counsel), believe will achieve the overall minimum in total combined present and reasonably anticipated future administrative expenses and taxes of all kinds. This applies not only to such Trust but also to its Beneficiaries, to the other Trusts hereunder and their Beneficiaries, and to the Grantor's Probate Estate.

Without limitation on the generality of the foregoing direction (which shall to that extent supersede the usual fiduciary duty of impartiality), such Fiduciaries shall not be accountable to any person interested in this Trust or to Grantor's Estate for the manner in which they shall carry out this direction to minimize overall taxes and expenses (including any decision they may make not to incur the expense of a detailed analysis of alternative choices). Even though their decisions in this regard may result in increased taxes or decreased distributions to the Trust, to the Estate, or to one or more Beneficiaries, the Fiduciaries shall not be obligated for compensation readjustments or reimbursements which arise by reason of the manner in which the Fiduciaries carry out this direction.

Section 6.03. Judgment and Discretion of Trustee

In the absence of proof of bad faith, all questions of construction or interpretation of any trusts created by this Trust Agreement will be finally and conclusively determined solely by the Trustee, according to the Trustee's best judgment and without recourse to any court, and each determination by the Trustee is binding on the Beneficiaries and prospective Beneficiaries hereunder, both in being and unborn, as well as all other persons, firms, or corporations. The Trustee, when exercising any discretionary power relating to the distribution or accumulation of principal or income or to the termination of any Trust, will be responsible only for lack of good faith in the exercise of such power. Each determination may be relied upon to the same extent as if it were a final and binding judicial determination. In the event of a conflict between the provisions of this Trust Agreement and those of the Michigan Statutes, the provisions of this Agreement will control.

Section 6.04. Trustee's Notice to Creditors

If no Personal Representative of Grantor's Estate has been appointed so that the publication and notice requirements with respect to creditors have not been discharged, Trustee shall, to the extent required by law, publish and serve notice to all creditors in the same manner as required for a Personal Representative. Trustee shall pay, to the extent required by law, all proper claims allowed by Trustee or a court having jurisdiction.

Section 6.05. Accountings and Information to Beneficiaries

Trustee's duty to inform and account to the Beneficiaries shall be governed by the following rules:

    A. Recipients of Information and Accountings
        1. As long as the Grantor is serving as a Trustee, the Trustee shall have no obligation to inform or account to anyone regarding the Trust and its administration.
        2. Prior to Grantor's death, if Grantor is not serving as a Trustee, Trustee shall, upon Grantor's written request, inform and account to Grantor regarding the Trust and its administration. However, during any period in which Grantor is incapacitated, Trustee shall inform and account to the following persons regarding the Trust and its administration:

a. the agent designated under Grantor's durable power of attorney then in effect, or if there is no person designated under a durable power of attorney who is acting as Grantor's agent, then

b. the then living current Trust Beneficiaries who are 18 years of age or older, are competent, and who are actually then receiving Trust distributions.

c. After Grantor's death, Trustee shall inform and account to the then living current Trust Beneficiaries who are 18 years of age or older who are competent and who are then actually receiving Trust distributions (other than tangible distributions of personal property) regarding the Trust and its administration.

B. Statement of Account—Trustee shall keep a true account of the affairs of the Trust. At least annually and upon termination of the Trust or a change of Trustee, Trustee shall (subject to the above provision entitled "Recipients of Information and Accountings") render an accounting that contains a concise description of the Trust purposes and the manner in which Trustee applied the Trust principal and income toward these purposes, and shows the receipts and disbursements made during the accounting period along with an inventory of the assets belonging to the Trust Estate at the beginning and end of the accounting period. The account may, in Trustee's sole discretion [as permitted by EPIC section 7303(3)] do any of the following: be stated in a manner and with terminology that is reasonably understandable, begin with a concise summary of its purpose and content, contain sufficient information to put interested persons on notice as to all significant transactions affecting administration during the accounting period, include both the carrying values (tax basis) and current values at the beginning and the end of the accounting period, show gains and losses incurred during the accounting period separately in the same schedule, and show significant transactions that do not affect the amount for which Trustee is accountable. The statement of account, if any, shall be delivered as soon as practicable after the close of the accounting period or upon the termination of the Trust or change of Trustee.

C. Inspection of Records—The books and records of Trustee relating to this Agreement shall be open at all reasonable times to inspection only by the current Trust Beneficiary or the current Trust Beneficiary's accredited representatives unless otherwise ordered by a court having jurisdiction; provided however during Grantor's lifetime only Grantor, or Grantor's designated agent if Grantor is incapacitated, shall have this right of inspection.

D. Settlement of Interim Accounts—Unless a Beneficiary acting individually or through a parent, the conservator of his or her estate, his or her nearest of kin, or an adult with whom he or she is living files with Trustee within 90 days after the accounting, written objection to an item contained in an account, to a fee claimed by Trustee or to reimbursable expenses, the accounting shall be deemed approved for all purposes and the amount of such fee or expenses shall be deemed reasonable.

E. Settlement of the Final Account—In the case of a final accounting, a receipt in full or a release by the Beneficiaries or by the conservator or other legal representative of those Beneficiaries who are disabled shall be binding, as to those Beneficiaries and as to all matters and transactions stated in the account or shown by it.

F. Court Approval of Account—Trustee is entitled at any time to have a judicial settlement of its account, and attorney fees, expenses, and other charges incident to the judicial proceeding may be charged against the Trust fund.

G. Delivery of Accountings—If the current Trust Beneficiary is another trust, the statement of account shall be delivered to the trustee of the other trust. If any current Trust Beneficiary is a minor or otherwise disabled, delivery shall be made to the conservator of his or her estate, or if none then to his or her parent, legal guardian, nearest of kin, or an adult with whom he or she is living. Trustee may deliver the statement of account to other Trust Beneficiaries at its discretion.

ARTICLE SEVEN

Section 7.01. Resolution of Conflict

Any controversy between the Trustee and any other Trustee or Trustees, or between any other parties to this Trust, including Beneficiaries, involving the construction or application of any of the terms, provisions, or conditions of this Trust shall, on the written request of either or any disagreeing party served on the other or others, be submitted to arbitration. The parties to such arbitration shall each appoint one person to hear and determine the dispute and, if they are unable to agree, then the two persons so chosen shall select a third impartial arbitrator whose decision shall be final and conclusive upon both parties. The cost of arbitration shall be borne by the losing party or in such proportion as the arbitrator(s) shall decide. Such arbitration shall comply with the commercial arbitration rules of the American Arbitration Association, New York Regional Office, 150 East 42nd Street, Floor 17, New York, NY 10017.

Section 7.02. Incontestability

The beneficial provisions of this Trust Agreement are intended to be in lieu of any other rights, claims, or interests of whatsoever nature, whether statutory or otherwise, except bona fide pre-death debts, which any Beneficiary hereunder may have in Grantor's Estate or in the properties in trust hereunder. Accordingly, if any Beneficiary hereunder asserts any claim (except a legally enforceable debt), statutory election, or other right or interest against or in Grantor's Estate, or any properties of this trust, other than pursuant to the express terms hereof, or directly or indirectly contests, disputes, or calls into question, before any court, the validity of this Trust Agreement, then:

a. Such Beneficiary shall thereby absolutely forfeit any and all beneficial interests of whatsoever kind and nature which such Beneficiary or his or her heirs might otherwise have under this Trust Agreement and the interests of the other Beneficiaries hereunder shall thereupon be appropriately and proportionately increased; and

b. All of the provisions of this Trust Agreement, to the extent that they confer any benefits, powers, or rights whatsoever upon such claiming, electing, or contesting Beneficiary, shall thereupon become absolutely void; and

c. Such claiming, electing, or contesting Beneficiary, if then acting as a Trustee hereunder, shall automatically cease to be a Trustee and shall thereafter be ineligible either to select, remove, or become a Trustee hereunder.

Section 7.03. Specific Omissions

Any and all persons and entities, except those persons and entities specifically named herein, have been intentionally omitted from this Trust Agreement. If any person or entity shall successfully challenge any term or condition of this Trust Agreement, then, to that person or entity shall be given the sum of one dollar ($1.00) in lieu and in place of any other benefit, grant, or interest which that person or interest may have in the Trust Estate.

ARTICLE EIGHT
Section 8.01. Distribution in Kind or Cash

On any division of the assets of the Trust Estate into shares or partial shares, and on any final or partial distribution of the assets of the Trust Estate, the Trustee, at his or her absolute discretion, may divide and distribute undivided interests of such assets on a pro rata or non-pro rata basis, or may sell all or any part of such assets and may make divisions or distributions in cash or partly in cash and partly in kind. The decision of the Trustee, either prior to or on any division or distribution of such assets, as to what constitutes a proper division of such assets of the Trust Estate shall be binding on all persons interested in any Trust provided for in this Trust Agreement.

Section 8.02. Spendthrift Provision

Neither the principal nor the income of the Trust shall be liable for the debts of a Beneficiary. Except as otherwise expressly provided in this Agreement, no Beneficiary of any Trust shall have any right, power, or authority to alienate, encumber, or hypothecate his or her interest in the principal or income of this Trust in any manner, nor shall the interests of any Beneficiary be subject to the claims of his or her creditors or liable to attachment, execution or other process of law. The limitations herein shall not restrict the exercise of any power of appointment or the right to disclaim.

Section 8.03. Definition of Children

The terms "child" and "children" as used in this Agreement mean the lawful issue of a Grantor or of the Grantors together. This definition also includes children legally adopted by a Grantor or by the Grantors together.

Section 8.04. Handicapped Beneficiaries

Any Beneficiary who is determined by a court of competent jurisdiction to be incompetent shall not have any discretionary rights of a Beneficiary with respect to this Trust, or to their share or portion thereof. The Trustee shall hold and maintain such incompetent Beneficiary's share of the Trust Estate and may, in the Trustee's sole discretion, provide for such Beneficiary as that Trustee would provide for a minor. Notwithstanding the foregoing, any Beneficiary who is diagnosed for the purposes of governmental benefits (as hereinafter delineated) as being not competent or as being disabled, and who shall be entitled to governmental support and benefits by reason of such incompetency or disability, shall cease to be a Beneficiary of this Trust. Likewise, they shall cease to be a Beneficiary if any share or portion of the principal or income of the Trust shall become subject to the claims of any governmental agency for costs or benefits, fees or charges.

The portion of the Trust Estate which, absent the provisions of this section, would have been the share of such incompetent or handicapped person shall be retained in trust for as long as that individual lives. The Trustee, at his or her sole discretion, shall utilize such funds for the maintenance of that individual. If such individual recovers from his or her incompetency or disability, and is no longer eligible for aid from any governmental agency, including costs or benefits, fees or charges, such individual shall be reinstated as a Beneficiary after 60 days from such recovery, and the allocation and distribution provisions as stated herein shall apply to that portion of the Trust Estate which is held by the Trustee subject to the foregoing provisions of this section. If said handicapped Beneficiary is no longer living and shall leave children then living, the deceased child's share shall pass to those children per stirpes. If there are no children, the share shall be allocated proportionately among the remaining Beneficiaries.

Section 8.05: Retirement Benefits

The following provisions concern Qualified Retirement Benefits that become distributable to the Trustees under this trust agreement by reason of the death of the Grantor(s). "Qualified Retirement Benefits" means amounts held in or payable pursuant to a plan qualified under Code Sec 408 or Code Sec 408A or a tax-sheltered annuity under Code Sec 403 or any other benefit subject to the distribution rules of Code Sec 401(a)(9).

A. Benefits Payable to Trustee—If Qualified Retirement Benefits are made payable to my estate or directly to the Trustees without specifying a particular Trustee, then the benefits shall be (unless specifically allocated to a particular Beneficiary) payable to the residuary Beneficiary(ies) in the proportions indicated.

B. Selection of Payout Schedule—The Trustees may in the Trustees' absolute discretion exercise any right to determine the manner and timing of payment of Qualified Retirement Benefits that is available to the recipient of the benefits, but they must exercise such rights in a manner consistent with the federal income tax rules regarding required distributions under Code Sec. 401(a)(9). However, if any Qualified Retirement Benefits are payable to a marital trust created herein, or to a spouse as the surviving Grantor of this trust, or to the trust and the spouse has survived and is a Grantor of this trust, the spouse shall have the absolute right in his or her individual capacity and absolute discretion, exercisable in all events, to withdraw from the plan, trust, or account from which the benefits are payable, all the income of the plan, trust, or account annually or at more frequent intervals. For this purpose, "income" means income as defined in Code Sec 643(b) determined as if the plan, trust, or account were a separate trust under this Trust Agreement.

C. Selection of "Designated Beneficiary"—The Trustees are authorized to identify and designate the person who is, under applicable provisions of the Code and Regulations, the "designated beneficiary" whose life expectancy may be used to measure payments to any trust. The Trustees may name as such designated beneficiary any individual to whom income, principal, or both may then be distributable under the other provisions of this Trust Agreement. Notwithstanding any other provision of this Trust Agreement, the Trustees shall promptly distribute to the Beneficiary, outright and free of trust, all amounts withdrawn by or distributed to the Trustees from any plan, trust, or account as to which such individual is the designated Beneficiary, and that are not otherwise distributable to such individual under other provisions of this trust agreement.

D. The Trustees in general are to take any action in distribution of the Trust to the designated beneficiaries of said plans or account or, if there are no specific designated beneficiaries to the Beneficiaries of this Trust Agreement so as not to incur any tax penalties regarding distributions to the extent possible and notwithstanding any other provisions herein, are authorized to amend this Trust for such purposes if necessary.

ARTICLE NINE
Section 9.01. Trustees
All Trustees are to serve without bond. Co-Trustees may divide their duties among themselves as they may agree. The following will act as Trustees of any Trusts created by this Trust Agreement, in the following order of succession:

First:	The undersigned, John Doe and/or Jane Doe.
Second:	The surviving spouse.
Third:	At the death or disability of both Grantors, Billie Jean Doe and Robert F. Doe shall serve as Successor Co-Trustees.
Fourth:	If either of them cannot act as Trustee, then the other shall serve as sole Successor Trustee.

Last: If there is no Trustee named above who is able or willing to act as Trustee, then a Trustee may be chosen by the majority of Beneficiaries, with a parent or legal guardian voting for minor Beneficiaries; provided, however, that the children of any deceased Beneficiary shall collectively have only one vote.

Trustees may be compensated if they choose at the customary rate paid to professional bank trustees for similar services. Trustees may divide their duties between themselves as they may agree in writing. Successor Trustees, absent written agreement, must unanimously agree on Trust decisions.

Section 9.02. Allocation and Distribution of the Trust Assets

The Trustees shall allocate, hold, administer, and distribute the Trust Assets as hereinafter provided:

a. Upon the death of the first Grantor, the Trustee shall make any separate distributions that have been specified by the deceased Grantor. The Trustee shall also take into consideration the appropriate provisions of this Article.

b. Upon the death of the surviving spouse, the Trustee shall hold, administer, and distribute the Trust Assets in the manner hereinafter prescribed.

Section 9.03. Personal Property Distribution

The Trustee must follow the directions of the Grantor as to the distribution of personal property attached as a signed or handwritten listing which is incorporated into this Trust Instrument, regarding the disposition of specific items of personal property or groups of personal property (for example, "All fishing equipment") of every kind including but not limited to furniture, appliances, furnishings, artwork, kitchenware, silverware, glass, books, jewelry, wearing apparel. Any personal property and household effects of the Grantors not listed shall be distributed pro rata in value in the same shares as all other Trust Assets. The Trustee shall decide on a method of dividing such unlisted assets such as selection by taking turns or by public auction or private sale. The list may be amended from time to time provided it is either notarized or written in the Grantor's handwriting.

Section 9.04. Liability of Trustee

The Trustee will not be responsible or liable for any loss which may occur by reason of depreciation in value of the properties at any time belonging to the Trust Estate, nor for any other loss which may occur, except that the Trustee will be liable for such Trustee's own negligence, neglect, default, or willful wrong. The Trustee will not be liable or responsible for the acts, omissions, or defaults of any agent or other person to whom duties may be properly delegated hereunder (except officers or regular employees of the Trustee) if such agent or person was appointed with due care. The Trustee may receive reimbursement from the Trust Estate for any liability, whether in contract or in tort, incurred in the administration of the Trust Estate in accordance with the provisions hereof, and the Trustee may contract in such form that such Trustee will be exempt from such personal liability and that such liability will be limited to the Trust Assets.

Section 9.05. Successor Trustees

Any Successor Trustee shall have all the power, rights, discretion, and obligations conferred on a Trustee by this Trust Agreement. All rights, titles, and interest in the property of the Trust shall immediately vest in the Successor Trustee at the time of appointment. The prior Trustee shall, without warranty, transfer to the Successor Trustee the existing Trust property. No Successor Trustee shall be under any duty to examine, verify, question, or audit the books, records, accounts, or transaction of any preceding Trustee; and no successor Trustee shall be liable or responsible in any way for any acts, defaults, or omissions of any predecessor Trustee, nor for any loss or expense from or occasioned by anything done or neglected to be done by any predecessor Trustee. A Successor Trustee shall be liable only for his or her own acts and defaults.

ARTICLE TEN

Section 10.01. Perpetuities Savings Clause

Notwithstanding any other provision of this instrument, the Trusts created hereunder shall terminate not later than twenty-one (21) years after the death of the last survivor of all Grantors and any other Beneficiary or Beneficiaries named or defined in this Trust living on the date of the death of the first spouse to die. The Trustee shall distribute each remaining Trust principal and all accrued or undistributed net income hereunder to the Beneficiary or Beneficiaries. If there is more than one Beneficiary, the distribution shall be in the proportion in which they are Beneficiaries; if no proportion is designated, then the distribution shall be in equal shares to such Beneficiaries

ARTICLE ELEVEN

Section 11.01. Governing Law

It is not intended that the laws of only one particular state shall necessarily govern all questions pertaining to all of the trust hereunder.

a. The validity of the Trust hereunder, as well as the validity of the particular provisions of that Trust, shall be governed by the laws of the state which has sufficient connection with this Trust to support such validity.
b. The meaning and effect of the terms of this Trust Agreement shall be governed by the laws of the State of Michigan.
c. The administration of this Trust shall be governed by the laws of the state in which the principal office of the Trustee then having custody of the Trust's principal assets and records is located.

The foregoing shall apply even though the situs of some Trust Assets or the home of the Grantor, a Trustee, or a Beneficiary may at some time or times be elsewhere.

Section 11.02. Invalidity of Any Provision
If a court finds that any provision of this Trust Agreement is void, invalid, or unenforceable, the remaining provisions of this Agreement will continue to be fully effective.

Section 11.03. Headings
The use of headings in connection with the various articles and sections of this Trust Agreement is solely for convenience, and the headings are to be given no meaning or significance whatever in construing the terms and provisions of this Agreement.

Section 11.04. Internal Revenue Code Terminology
As used herein, the words "gross estate," "adjusted gross estate," "taxable estate," "unified credit," "state death tax credit," "maximum marital deduction," "marital deduction," and any other word or words which from the context in which it or they are used to refer to the Internal

Revenue Code shall be assigned the same meaning as such words have for the purposes of applying the Internal Revenue Code to a deceased Grantor's Estate. Reference to sections of the Internal Revenue Code and to the Internal Revenue Code shall refer to the Internal Revenue Code amended to the date of such Grantor's death.

Dated to be effective this _____ day of _____, 20_____.

GRANTORS/TRUSTEES:

_____
John Doe

_____
Jane Doe

STATE OF _____
COUNTY OF _____

On this the _____ day of _____, 20_____: Before me, a Notary Public, personally appeared John H. Doe and Jane Doe, personally known to me, or who provided _____ as identification to be the person whose name is subscribed to this instrument, and acknowledged that he executed it for the purposes herein expressed.

_____
(Notary Public Signature)

(Seal)

Sample Pour-Over Will

LAST WILL AND TESTAMENT
(Pour-Over Will)
of
John H. Doe

IDENTITY

I, John H. Doe of 1234 Elm Street, Anytown, Michigan, being of sound mind and memory, and not acting under duress or undue influence of any person whomsoever, hereby declare this to be my Last Will and Testament, and I do hereby revoke all other and former Wills and Codicils to Wills heretofore made by me.

DEBTS, TAXES, AND ADMINISTRATION EXPENSES

I have provided for the payment of all my debts, expenses of administration of property wherever situated passing under this Will or otherwise, and estate, inheritance, transfer, and succession taxes, other than any tax on a generation-skipping transfer that is not a liability of my Estate (including interest and penalties, if any) that become due by reason of my death, under the John H. Doe Revocable Living Trust executed on even date herewith (the "Revocable Trust"). If the Revocable Trust assets should be insufficient for these purposes, my Personal Representative shall pay any unpaid items from the residue of my Estate passing under this Will, without any apportionment or reimbursement. In the alternative, my Personal Representative may demand in a writing addressed to the Trustee of the Trust an amount necessary to pay all or part of these items, plus claims, pecuniary legacies, and family allowances by court order.

PERSONAL AND HOUSEHOLD EFFECTS

It is my intent that all my personal and household effects were transferred to the Revocable Trust as a result of the assignment form signed this date. If there are any questions regarding the ownership or disposition of these assets, it is my desire that such assets pour into the Revocable Trust, signed by me this date in accordance with the provisions of the section titled "Residue of Estate."

RESIDUE OF ESTATE

I give, devise, and bequeath all the rest, residue, and remainder of my property of every kind and description (including lapsed legacies and devises), wherever situated and whether acquired before or after the execution of this Will, to the Trustee under that certain Trust executed by me on the same date of the execution of this Will. The Trustee shall add the property bequeathed and devised by this item to the corpus of the above described Trust and shall hold, administer, and distribute said property in accordance with the provisions of the said Trust, including any amendments thereto made before my death.

If for any reason the said Trust shall not be in existence at the time of my death, or if for any reason a court of competent jurisdiction shall declare the foregoing testamentary disposition to the Trustee under said Trust as it exists at the time of my death to be invalid, then I give all of my Estate including the residue and remainder thereof to that person who would have been the Trustee under the Trust, as Trustee, and to their substitutes and successors under the Trust, described hereinabove, to be held, managed, invested, reinvested, and distributed by the Trustee upon the terms and conditions pertaining to the period beginning with the date of my death as are constituted in the Trust as at present constituted giving effect to amendments, if any, hereafter made and for that purpose I do hereby incorporate such Trust by reference into this my Will.

PERSONAL REPRESENTATIVE

I hereby nominate and appoint Billie Jean Doe and Robert F. Doe as my Independent Personal Representatives of this my Last Will and Testament to serve without bond.

Whenever the word "Personal Representative" or any modifying or substituted pronoun therefor is used in this my Will, such words and respective pronouns shall be held and taken to include both the singular and the plural, the masculine, feminine, and neutral gender thereof and shall apply equally to the Personal Representative named herein and to any successor or substitute Personal Representative acting hereunder, and such successor or substitute Personal Representative shall possess all the rights, powers, duties, authority, and responsibility conferred upon the Personal Representative originally named herein.

PERSONAL REPRESENTATIVE POWERS

By way of illustration and not of limitation and in addition to any inherent, implied or statutory powers granted to Personal Representatives generally, my Personal Representative is specifically authorized and empowered with respect to any property, real or personal, at any time held under any provision of this my Will: to allot, allocate between principal and income, assign, borrow, buy, care for, collect, compromise claims, contract with respect to, continue any business of mine, convey, convert, deal with, dispose of, enter into, exchange, hold, improve, incorporate any business of mine, invest, lease, manage, mortgage, grant and exercise options with respect to, take possession of, pledge, receive, release, repair, sell, sue for, make distributions in cash or in kind or partly in each without regard to the income tax basis of such asset and in general, exercise all of the powers in the management of my Estate which any individual could exercise in the management of similar property owned in its own right upon such terms and conditions as to my Personal Representative may deem best, and execute and deliver any and all instruments and do all acts which my Personal Representative may deem proper or necessary to carry out the purpose of this my Will, without being limited in any way by the specific grants or power made, and without the necessity of a court order.

My Personal Representative shall have absolute discretion, but shall not be required, to make adjustments in the rights of any Beneficiaries, or among the principal and income accounts to compensate for the consequences of any tax decision or election, or of any investment or administrative decision, that my Personal Representative believes has had the effect, directly or indirectly, of preferring one Beneficiary or group of Beneficiaries over others. In determining the federal estate and income tax liabilities of my Estate, my Personal Representative shall have discretion to select the valuation date and to determine whether any or all of the allowable administration expenses in my Estate shall be used as federal estate tax deductions or as federal income tax deductions.

SPECIFIC OMISSIONS

I have intentionally omitted any and all persons and entities from this, my Last Will and Testament, except those persons and entities specifically named herein. If any person or entity shall challenge any term or condition of this Will, or of the Living Trust to which I have made reference in the sections "Household and Personal Effects" and "Residue of Estate," then to that person or entity I give and bequeath the sum of one dollar ($1.00) only in lieu and in place of any other benefit, grant, bequest, or interest which that person or interest may have in my Estate or the Living Trust and its Estate.

SIMULTANEOUS DEATH

If any Beneficiary should not survive me for sixty (60) days, then it shall be conclusively presumed purposes of this my Will that said Beneficiary predeceased me.

This instrument consists of 6 typewritten pages including this one. This instrument is being signed by me on this _____ day of _____, 20_____.

_____
John H. Doe

ATTESTATION CLAUSE

This document, consisting of 6 pages, was signed by John H. Doe in our presence and was declared by to be his Last Will and Testament and we therefore sign our names in each other's presence as witnesses thereto.

WITNESSES:

_____   _____
(Signature)   (Signature)

_____   _____
(Printed Name of Witness)   (Printed Name of Witness)

_____   _____
(Address)   (Address)

_____   _____
(City, State, Zip Code)   (City, State, Zip Code)

STATE OF _____
COUNTY OF _____

On this the _____ day of _____
20_____: Before me a Notary Public, personally appeared John H. Doe, personally known to me or who provided _____ as identification to be the person whose name is subscribed to this instrument, and acknowledged that he executed it for the purposes herein expressed.

_____
(Notary Public Signature)

(Seal)

Sample Assignment of Assets to Trust

The undersigned hereby declares that solely as trustee of and for the benefit of the revocable trust executed by the grantor and by the initial trustee, which is more precisely described as the John H. Doe Revocable Trust Agreement dated _____ day of _____ 20 _____ and under the provisions of said trust agreement, the undersigned is now holding and will hold solely and exclusively for and on behalf of such trust, the following: any and all properties of all kinds, whether presently owned or hereafter acquired (regardless of the name by which acquired) including, without limitation:

Bank accounts, certificates of deposit, mutual and money market funds of all kinds, securities, agency and custody accounts, notes, real estate wherever located (including mortgages, contract for deed interests, leaseholds, and mineral interests), jewelry, antiques, and any and all other assets wherever located and any replacement or additional property acquired in the future. All such property is hereby transferred to and the same shall be owned by such trust.

This declaration shall apply even though record ownership or title, in some instances, may, presently or in the future, be registered in the individual name in which event such record of ownership shall hereafter be deemed held in trust even though such trusteeship remains undisclosed. The terms of this assignment are severable so that the disallowance of part shall not affect the validity of those articles remaining. This assignment is not intended to affect or sever rights of tenants by the entirety in real estate.

The undersigned hereby affirms and declares that from and after the date hereof:

1. All properties described above will be held by the undersigned exclusively for and on behalf of said trust as true owners (subject to any and all instructions from the trustee of said trust), and

2. Except to the extent of beneficial interests provided to the undersigned, under the terms and provisions of said trust (as now written and as the same may in the future be amended), the undersigned has and shall have no personal interest in any of the properties described above, and

3. All liabilities which relate in any way to the acquisition of, or which are a lien upon, any of the properties governed by this declaration shall be borne by the trust which, pursuant to this assignment, owns such properties.

This assignment is intended to be and shall be binding upon the undersigned's heirs, legal representatives, and assigns and shall be revocable only by written instrument executed by the undersigned.

WHEREFORE, I hereby execute this Assignment of assets to trust this _____ day of _____, 20_____.

GRANTOR:

_____

John H. Doe

_____   _____
(Witness Signature)   (Witness Signature)

_____   _____
(Witness Printed Name)   (Witness Printed Name)

STATE OF _____

COUNTY OF _____

On this the _____ day of _____ 20_____:
Before me a Notary Public, personally appeared John H. Doe, personally known to me or who provided _____
_____ as identification to be the person whose name is subscribed to this instrument, and acknowledged that he executed it for the purposes herein expressed.

_____
(Notary Public Signature)

(Seal)

Glossary of Terms

administrator: A person appointed by a court to be in charge of a probated estate. This is in cases where there is no one appointed in a will to act as executor or personal representative. The title *administratrix* is a word rarely used to refer to a female who is appointed in that role. If there is a will, the person is called an executor or personal representative.

affidavit: A written statement under oath that has been notarized and sometimes witnessed.

ancillary probate: A probate proceeding in a state different from a decedent's state of residence because there are assets, typically real estate, owned by the decedent located in that other state. Ancillary probate is required in each state where a person owns real estate unless the owner has a probate-avoiding, properly funded estate plan.

beneficiary: A person who is named to inherit from a deceased person through a will, trust, deed, insurance, or investment account.

bequest: Property other than real estate left to someone by will.

bond: A type of insurance policy to cover any losses to an estate because of the negligence or malfeasance of a person in charge of the assets or a person or estate. Sometimes called a surety bond.

codicil: A written amendment to a will signed with the same statutory requirements as a will.

community property: In certain states, all property acquired during a marriage and property comingled with separate property of each spouse, except certain separately owned property and inherited property, and except as agreed to in writing by both spouses, is presumed to be owned by both spouses equally.

creditor: A person, company, or other legal entity who is owed money or other assets by the decedent.

decedent: The person who has died—the deceased.

deed: A written document that legally transfers a parcel of real estate to another person or legal entity. State law spells out the format and other legal requirements that must be followed to make the document legally binding and effective.

devise: Real estate left to another by the last will and testament of the decedent.

escheat: A procedure in which the assets of a decedent are transferred to the state because there are no known heirs of the decedent.

estate: The totality of the assets owned by a decedent at the time of his or her death.

estate recovery: A state law that allows the state to claim repayment of government benefits, such as Medicaid for nursing home care, from a deceased person's probated estate.

estate tax: The federal tax on the taxable portion of a decedent's estate.

executor: The person named in a will to administer the probate of a decedent. Rarely used is the term *executrix* referring to a female acting in the same role.

grantor: The person who creates a trust. Also called a settlor or trustor.

heir: A person who is entitled to receive the assets of a decedent either by operation of law, beneficiary designation (or POD/TOD designation), a bequest or devise in a will, or as a named person or institution in a trust.

heirs at law: Those people who, by statute, are the heirs of a decedent in order of the laws of descent and distribution. For example, an unmarried person's children who survive him are his or her heirs at law and share equally in his estate if there is no will. If there are no children, his grandchildren inherit, and if no grandchildren, then his parents are his heirs. If there are no surviving parents, then his siblings are next in line. State laws might vary, and at some point in tracing relatives, the laws stop descending, and the person is said to have no heirs at law and thus is subject to escheat to the state. See chapter 1.

holographic will: A handwritten or hand-acknowledged will, often signed without witnesses. It is valid in many states and is usually put in front of a judge to ratify it as a legal last will and testament.

inheritance tax: A state tax assessed against the value of an estate exceeding a certain threshold set out by law. Not all states assess an inheritance tax.

intangible property. Includes such things as bank deposits, accounts, partnership interests, brokerage accounts, patents, software, and other things of value which do not have a physical presence.

inter vivos trust: A living trust.

intestate: An estate of a person who had no will.

intestate succession: A list of the heirs of a person who died without a will in order of priority based upon their family relationship to the deceased. See descent and distribution.

inventory: A list of all the assets in a probated estate and their values. This is used as a basis for assessing inventory fees paid to the court.

irrevocable trust: A trust that cannot be changed after it takes effect except in limited circumstances. Some trusts begin as revocable trusts but become partially or wholly revocable in the future, such as a revocable living trust, which becomes irrevocable at the death of the grantor.

issue: The lineal blood-related descendants of a person. Children and grandchildren.

joint tenancy: A form of legal ownership, usually meaning that they all own the property equally, not separate shares. In most cases it means that if one joint owner dies, his or her share goes to the surviving owners. To avoid confusion, the words "with right of survivorship" are added.

personal property: Tangible assets other than real estate and intangibles. Things such as furniture, sporting goods, clothing, tools and equipment, and such. I like to call it your "stuff."

personal representative: The role of a person in charge of a probated estate, formerly and sometimes called an executor. This person is usually nominated through a will but is always approved by a court.

POD: An acronym for "pay on death." Used as a type of beneficiary designation on investment or retirement accounts. Similar to and sometimes used synonymously with TOD, transfer on death.

pour-over will: A will in which the beneficiary is the willmaker's trust rather than an individual, so that the trust distributes all probated assets according to the trust directions and restrictions.

pretermitted heir: An heir at law who is not mentioned in a will or who was born after the will was made and who takes his or her intestate share by operation of law.

probate: The court-supervised process of validating a will, appointing a personal representative, and administering a decedent's estate through the collection of assets, determination of heirs, approving payment to creditors, collection of fees and taxes due to the state, resolution of conflicting claims, and distribution of assets to the heirs. If there is no will the process is almost exactly the same.

real property: Real estate. As opposed to personal property and intangible property.

revocable trust: A trust that can be changed according to the terms of its provisions. It usually becomes irrevocable upon the death of the grantor or upon her legal disability. A trust might also be revoked, typically by removing all assets from the trust name, changing beneficiary designations away from the trust, and revoking or destroying the pour-over will.

right of survivorship: In co-owned property, at the death of one owner, that share automatically belongs to the other co-owners.

successor trustee: The person appointed to take the place of a named trustee in a trust who is either unable to act as trustee or who dies, resigns, or refuses to act as trustee.

summary probate: A short-form or expedited probate of various kinds in different states to transfer assets from the deceased to the rightful heirs without court proceedings. Usually for smaller and simpler estates.

tenants by the entirety: Assets owned by a husband and wife jointly. Similar to joint tenants with right of survivorship but with other rights that are assigned to the spouses as well as additional or different requirements in transferring the joint assets.

tenants in common: A type of joint ownership where each co-owner owns a separate share of the whole. That separate share can be sold, mortgaged, transferred, or devised by will without the consent of the other owners, and at the death of a tenant in common that share is part of his or her estate, so there is no right of survivorship.

testate: Having signed a valid will.

testator: The person who signs his or her will.

TOD: An acronym for "transfer on death." A type of beneficiary designation that transfers the asset, usually a bank or deposit account, to a named person without probate. Sometimes TOD and POD are used interchangeably, so you might occasionally see a TOD deed.

trust: A legal document, which, when signed, creates a legal entity—a legal person, if you will—that has the authority to own assets, manage them for the benefit of the trust beneficiaries, and continue carrying out its provisions after the death or disability of the trust grantor. It might be required to file its own tax returns. The rights, powers, and duties of the trust are set out in state law, common law, and the text of the document itself.

trustee: The person or persons who are in charge of a trust and who carry on its business and follow the directions set out in the trust document as to management of assets and distributions of the trust to named trust beneficiaries. The trustee is normally appointed in the trust document but might also be appointed by a judge or by the process described in the trust itself.

will: A written document directing who gets a decedent's estate, who is in charge of the probate of the estate, and written according to specific requirements of language, witnessing, and signing.

will safe: Attorneys sometimes hold an original signed will in their office for safekeeping and turn it over to the named personal representative or to the court upon the death of the will maker. This often results in the attorney being hired to probate the will. It's usually a filing cabinet, not a safe.

Index

 **Books from Allworth Press**

Estate Planning for the Healthy, Wealthy Family
by Carla Garrity, Mitchell Baris, and Stanley Neeleman (6 × 9, 256 pages, ebook, $22.99)

Estate Planning (in Plain English)®
by Leonard D. DuBoff and Amanda Bryan (6 × 9, 240 pages, paperback, $19.99)

Feng Shui and Money (Second Edition)
by Eric Shaffert (6 × 9, 256 pages, paperback, $19.99)

How to Plan and Settle Estates
by Edmund Fleming (6 × 9, 288 pages, paperback, $16.95)

Legal Forms for Everyone (Sixth Edition)
by Carl Battle (8½ × 11, 280 pages, paperback, $24.99)

Living Trusts for Everyone (Second Edition)
by Ronald Farrington Sharp (5½ × 8¼, 192 pages, paperback $14.99)

Legal Guide to Social Media
by Kimberly A. Houser (6 × 9, 208 pages, paperback, $19.95)

Love & Money
by Ann-Margaret Carrozza with foreword by Dr. Phil McGraw (6 × 9, 240 pages, paperback, $19.99)

The Money Mentor
by Tad Crawford (6 × 9, 272 pages, paperback, $24.95)

Protecting Your Assets from Probate and Long-Term Care
by Evan H. Farr (6 × 9, 208 pages, paperback, $14.99)

Scammed
by Gini Graham Scott, PhD (6 × 9, 256 pages, paperback, $14.99)

The Secret Life of Money
by Tad Crawford (5½ × 8½, 304 pages, paperback, $19.95)

The Smart Consumer's Guide to Good Credit
by John Ulzheimer (5¼ × 8¼, 216 pages, paperback, $14.95)

Your Living Trust & Estate Plan (Fifth Edition)
by Harvey J. Platt (6 × 9, 352 pages, paperback, $16.95)

To see our complete catalog or to order online, please visit *www.allworth.com*.